T0036755

A Kid's Guide to Plants of the Pacific Northwest

A Kid's Guide to Plants of the Pacific Northwest

with Cool Facts, Activities and Recipes

Philippa Joly

HARBOUR PUBLISHING

Table of Contents

Author's Note

This book was written on the K'ómoks, Pentlatch, Qualicum, Homalco, Klahoose, Tla'amin, We Wai Kai and Wei Wai Kum lands where I live. It was dreamed up on the Lekwungen, W̱SÁNEĆ, Musqueam, Squamish and Tsleil-Waututh lands where I have lived in the past. I am indebted to all the Indigenous knowledge keepers who have taught me what I know about plants, directly and indirectly. I hold in my heart the complex historical and ongoing displacement of Indigenous people from their lands, and the destruction of the land, as I work with the plants of these lands. I thank, also, my own ancestors for carrying the knowledge they have through many eras of their own displacement. This book is dedicated to the plants themselves. May they always be wild and free.

Safety First!

This book contains information about plants you can eat and plants you cannot eat. There are some very poisonous plants on the Pacific Northwest Coast. It is very important that anyone using this book and eating wild plants be sure of what they are eating. Before you eat any plant in the wild, check with a knowledgeable adult to make sure it is safe to eat. There are also activities in this book that must be done with the help of an adult. This is to keep you safe. The author and the publisher are not liable in the unlikely chance you get hurt by eating wild plants or doing an activity with them. Stay curious and stay safe.

Katrina Rainoshek

Katrina Rainoshek

Katrina Rainoshek

Katrina Rainoshek

Introduction

What's So Cool about Plants Anyway?

People often ask me how I first got interested in plants. I tell them about my older sister. I always thought she was pretty cool, and I wanted to be like her. One day when she was about sixteen and I was fourteen, she came back from a trip she went on with a friend to some little island where there was no electricity or paved roads. I was jealous. I wanted to go too, but I was too young. I asked what she did there, and she told me all about a class about plants she had taken with a woman with a name like River or Waterfall or Ocean. "Look," my sister said, pointing at a little plant at our feet. "That one is called Yellow Dock, or *Rumex crispus*. You can eat it." It was in that moment that a light went on inside me. There was something captivating about those words: *Rumex crispus*. They sounded like magic. I repeated those words, *Rumex crispus*, to myself over and over as I delved into my fascination with plants that has now lasted over twenty-six years. And I still look up to my big sister, even if I am half an inch taller than she is.

You may not have a big sister or ever have heard such weird-sounding words as *Rumex crispus*, but you probably

At Salix School, we nibble the fresh leaves of Oregon Grape, we make crowns out of Willow and we get so muddy tracking raccoons that one kid said, "I'm so dirty, my mom is going to kill me! This is awesome!"

Learn New Words

. . . .

When words are in **this font** it means they are in the Glossary on page 206. Look there to learn the meaning of words you don't know!

A learning moment at Salix School.

Katrina Rainoshek

have your own story about plants. No matter who you are or where you live, plants are a big part of our lives. Plants are the food we eat. Bread is made from wheat, which is a grass. Cotton is grown to spin into fabric to make clothing. Paper we use at school is made from trees. Some fuel we put in our cars is made from corn. Much of our medicine is or was once made from plants. We play on grass lawns and twirl "helicopter seeds" dropped from trees. These are all ways we have relationships with plants. Can you imagine a world without them?!

Plants are everywhere. If you live in a city, Dandelions pushing up through the cracks in the sidewalk remind us of the strength of one little seed. Weeds like Wild Carrot and Thistle have long roots that help break up hard, compacted

earth. Trees line the streets, there are roses in your neighbour's garden and your grandma grows peas on her little balcony. For those of you who don't live in the city, there are so many plants that you may almost not even notice them. They may just blur into a wall of green.

In our world today, kids spend a lot of time inside on screens or in scheduled activities. Many kids don't know the names of the plants around them. Maybe you can win at a video game, but would you know what to eat in the woods? Learning about plants might seem like a waste of time when you have homework to do or a snap to send. But with an uncertain future due to climate change and a natural world that needs caring for, knowing about plants can change—and maybe even save—your life.

When the pandemic first hit and people were hoarding all the toilet paper, would you like to have known which plant makes a good replacement? If you are hungry, it would be good to know which plants you could eat and which are poisonous. And have you ever had a lonely, terrible day when you felt like you had no one to talk to? Plants are always there to listen.

Plants want to be known. For as long as there have been humans, we have had relationships with plants. Find your favourite abandoned lot, community garden, **old-growth forest**, creekside, park or backyard, and start there. Choose

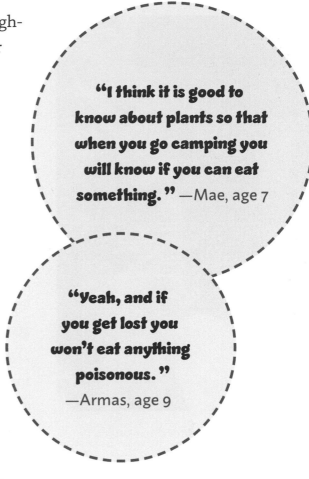

"I think it is good to know about plants so that when you go camping you will know if you can eat something." —Mae, age 7

"Yeah, and if you get lost you won't eat anything poisonous." —Armas, age 9

Arawyn taking notes on Sword Fern.

How many pop songs do you know all the words to? Now, how many bird songs do you know?

a plant or two and find out who they are, what they might be good for, what makes them special. Just like you and me, every plant is unique and has something to offer. The more we know about plants, the more we care about them. This care then leads us to care for the place these plants live.

One of the reasons I love my work is that I get to spend so much time outside around plants. I run a nature school where kids get to have fun interacting with plants and the land around them. We get to do things like eat wild foods, walk across logs over creeks, learn to identify bird calls, practise our animal tracking skills, find animal kill sites and learn to feel more at home in the outdoors. There are nature schools in many cities and towns all up and down the West Coast. If you are interested in going to one, just look online for "nature schools where I live."

I also work as a herbalist, which means I harvest wild plants, make them into medicine and then help people who are sick get better using the healing powers of plants. Just like in the old days, before there were doctors and drug companies, there were people who knew which plant to give someone for a cold, which plant would stop bleeding and which plant would help with aches and pains. Plants are very generous; they don't ask for money. The only thing they ask is that we keep where they live healthy and treat them with respect. We can all relate to that!

This book is written in the hope that you will learn to love plants and the places where they grow. There are lots of ideas for games and activities that you can do with the plants so that you are not just learning their names, but also forming a relationship with them. You can share this book with the adults in your life, and you may need an adult's help to do some of the activities. If your adults are interested in learning more about plants, there's a section just for them at the back of the book.

I wrote this book from my perspective, which is the only perspective I know. I grew up in Victoria, on Songhees/Lekwungen territory, where I learned to love the plants of that area. My skin is white and my ancestors are from France and Scotland. Although I know a lot about the plants in this area, I will never know as much as someone whose family has been on this land since time immemorial (that means longer than anyone can remember). I am honoured to have learned about plants from people who have spent time with Indigenous Elders and then shared that information with me. I have tried to make my sharing about plants as respectful as possible.

Now, go outside and say hi to the first plant you see. It is waiting to tell you all about itself. Then see if you can find it in this book. See you outside!

Can you find Naomi doing a backbend on the giant nurse log?

Indigenous Peoples of the Pacific Northwest Coast

There are people from all over the world who now live on the west coast of what is called North America. But not that long ago, only about 250 years ago, there were only **Indigenous** people who lived here. What changed?

Since time immemorial, people have lived on the Pacific Northwest Coast in ways that are connected to the land, the seasons and the plants. People with distinct cultures and languages. For example, there are Haida people in Haida Gwaii, W̱SÁNEĆ people in Saanich, Quw'utsun people in Duncan, Stó:lō people in the Fraser Canyon, Lekwungen people in Victoria and Musqueam people in Vancouver. Before European contact, Indigenous people needed plants for their lives: for food, clothing, medicine, canoes, houses, fire, tools, fishing, hunting and spiritual connection. Because they relied on plants so much, they didn't waste plants or cut them all down. They lived in a relationship with the plants, treating them as family and with respect. Many Indigenous people still do this today.

In the 1770s, Spanish explorers sailed up the coast of what would later be called Vancouver Island. They brought things that the Indigenous people of the Coast hadn't seen before, like metal cooking pots, steel knives and glass beads. They also brought sicknesses that the Coastal people had never had. These sicknesses killed a lot of people, and when the French and British people came for furs and gold in the 1800s, they brought more sickness. Of the approximately 100,000 Indigenous people on the Coast, 95 percent died from illnesses that were brought by the colonizers. That means out of every one hundred people, only five were alive after **colonization**.

When so many people die, it is hard to keep culture, language and stories alive, but people did and still do. Those who lost a lot of their relatives moved in with other families, and eventually people formed new villages. With so many people dead, many villages were empty, which made it easier for the new settlers coming from Europe to take the land that was not theirs. The Coastal Indigenous people were then forced to live on very small reserves of land, and their children were taken away and put into residential schools. Despite this very difficult history, which still affects Indigenous people every day, there are strong, thriving and reviving Indigenous cultures up and down the Coast today.

When we read about Indigenous people in books, it is often in the past tense: "People *relied* on Cedar for many important parts of their culture." Instead, we should say "People *rely* on Cedar for many important parts of their

Gathering Digii (black huckleberries) in Wet'suwet'en territory. Molly Wickham

Whini picking Digii (Black Huckleberries). Molly Wickham

culture." Not only are Indigenous people not just in the past, but many of them still rely on plants and trees in their culture today. There are many Coastal Indigenous people who use plants every day and who are helping to connect Indigenous and non-Indigenous people to the wonderful and generous world of plants. Barb Whyte, a Pentlatch/ K'ómoks Elder who lives in the Comox Valley, shares a lot about local plants. She even teaches kids in schools what wild plants make yummy teas. And Wet'suwet'en Land and Water Defender Molly Wickham gathers plants with her kids to keep them connected to their homelands.

An important part of working with plants is forming a relationship with the land where you live. Learning whose traditional territory you live on or what Indigenous nation lives where you live is one step toward honouring the people whose land you are on and their ancestors who tended it. Much of what we know about the uses of plants on the Coast has come to us from the Elders of the Coastal Indigenous cultures. This is important to remember for two reasons. First, recognition of who our teachers are, even if we are learning about the plants through books, helps keep alive respect for the traditions and the cultures that support them. Second, because we live and learn on land that has been tended and shaped by thousands of years of Coastal Indigenous cultures, even if those cultures are not visible to us now, we are always on Indigenous land.

Indigenous Territories of the Coastal Pacific Northwest

This graphic is based on information from https://native-land.ca —you can go online to learn more about the traditional territory where you live.

Alaska

Yukon

British Columbia

Washington

Oregon

California

1 ALASKA
Eyak
Haida
Lingít Aaní (Tlingit)

BRITISH COLUMBIA

2 Northern Coast
Gitga'at Lax Yuup
Gitxaała
Haida
hiłzaqv ẁáẃís (Heiltsuk)
Kitselas
Kitsumkalum
Lax Kw'Alaams
Lax̱yuubm Ts'msyen (Tsimshian)
Nisga'a
Tā̀ltān Konelīne (Tahltan)
x̱à'isla ẃáẃís (Haisla)

3 Central Coast
Gwa'Sala-'Nakwaxda'xw
hiłzaqv ẁáẃís (Heiltsuk)
Kulhulmcilh (Nuxalk)
Kwakwaka'wakw A̱wi'nagwis
Wuikinuxv (Oweekeno)

4 Southern Coast and Vancouver Island
Á,LEṈEṈEȻ ȽTE (W̱SÁNEĆ)
BOḰEĆEN (Pauquachin)
Cayuse, Umatilla and
    Walla Walla
Da'naxda'xw Awaetlatla
ditidaqiičaq disiba?k (Ditidaht)
Gwa'Sala-'Nakwaxda'xw
Halalt
Hesquiaht
Homalco
Hul'qumi'num Treaty Group
Hupacasath
Huu-ay-aht
K'ómoks
Ka:'yu:'k't'h'/Che:k'tles7et'h'
Kwakwaka'wakw A̱wi'nagwis
Kwantlen

Kwiakah
kʷikʷəƛ̓əm
ła?amɪn gɪǰe (Tla'amin)
Lekwungen/Songhees
Liǧʷiłdax̌ʷ
Lhaq'temish (Lummi)
ƛaʔuukʷiʔatḥ (Tla-o-qui-aht)
ƛohos giǰi (Klahoose)
MÁLEXEȽ (Malahat)
Musgamagw Dzawada'enuxw
nuučaańuuɫ?atḥ nism̓a
    (Nuu-chah-nulth)
Nuwhaha
Pacheedaht
Qayqayt
Quatsino
Quw'utsun
S'Klallam
S'ólh Téméxw (Stó:lō)
Sc'ianew
sćəwaθena?ɫ təməxʷ
    (Tsawwassen)
Semiahmoo
səl̓ilwəta?ɫ təməxʷ
    (Tsleil-Waututh)
shíshálh swíya (Sechelt)
Skwxwú7mesh-ulh
    Temíx̱w (Squamish)
Snaw-naw-as
Snuneymuxw
sq̓əc̓iy̓aʔɫ təməxʷ (Katzie)
Stz'uminus
šx̌ʷməθkʷəy̓əma?ɫ təməxʷ
    (Musqueam)
Te'mexw Treaty Association
Toquaht
Ts'uubaa-asatx
Tseshaht
Uchucklesaht
We Wai Kai
We Wai Kum
W̱JOȽEȽP (Tsartlip)
W̱SÍḴEM (Tseycum)
Yuułu?ił?atḥ

5 WASHINGTON
Cayuse, Umatilla and
    Walla Walla
ChalAt'i'lo t'sikAti (Chalat')
Chinook
Chimacum
Clatsop-Nehalem
    Confederated Tribes
Confederated Tribes of
    Grand Ronde
Confederated Tribes of
    Siletz Indians
Hul'qumi'num Treaty Group
Kathlamet
KiKiallus
Konnaack
Lekwungen/Songhees
Lhaq'temish (Lummi)
Lower Chinook
Nuwhaha
Nuxwsa'7aq (Nooksack)
Nłe?kepmx Tmíxʷ
    (Nlaka'pamux)
Pacheedaht
Queets
Quileute
Quinault
Qʷidičča?a•tx̌ (Makah)
Sauk Suiattle
Samish
Semiahmoo
Skagit
S'Klallam
Shoalwater Bay
Snohomish
Sq'ʷayáiłaqtmš (Chehalis)
Suquamish
Stl'pulmsh (Cowlitz)
Stillaguamish
Stz'uminus
Swinomish
Tulalip
Wahkiakum
Willapa

6 OREGON &
NORTHERN CALIFORNIA
Älsé (Alsea)
Bear River
Cahto
Cayuse, Umatilla and
    Walla Walla
Central Pomo
Chilula
Chinook
Chit-dee-ni (Chetco)
Clatsop-Nehalem
    Confederated Tribes
Coast Yuki
Confederated Tribes of
    Grand Ronde
Confederated Tribes of
    Siletz Indians
Coos, Lower Umpqua, Siuslaw
Hanis Coos
Kathlamet
Konnaack
Mattole
Miluk Coos
Nehalem
Nestucca
Nongatl
Northern Pomo
Quuiich (Lower Umpqua)
Resighini Rancheria (Yurok)
Salmon River
Siletz
Sinkyone
Siuslaw
Tillamook
Tolowa Dee-ni'
Tututni
Wahkiakum
Whilkut
Wiyot
Yakina
Yurok

Regions and Plants Covered by This Book

The term *Pacific Northwest* commonly refers to an area from Northern California to Southern Alaska and from the Pacific Coast to the Coast Mountains that has shared plant and animal **species**. In this book, I refer to this region simply as "the Coast," as this is how it is frequently referred to by those of us who live here. Of course, there are many other "Coasts" in the world, like the East Coast or the Gulf Coast of Mexico, for example.

The Coast is home to a wide range of plant and animal species that have adapted to live here and to live together, like Deer Mice and Douglas Fir trees. Many of the plants and animals who live here have been here since the last glaciers receded from the land 10,000 years ago. They are well suited to the dry summers and the wet winters. For example, Licorice Fern can die back in the dry summer and then thrive in the wet winter. We are lucky to share this beautiful place with many rare and special plants, like Camas Lilies and Ghost Pipe. This is one of the last places in the world with areas of almost intact forests and ancient trees that provide **ecosystems** and **habitat** for many special plants and animals. In fact, biologists and forest activists are still finding new species of plants and animals in the remaining scraps of old-growth forests on the Coast.

This book focuses on common plants that you can meet in many places—in forests, by the ocean, by marshes and even in cities. There are a few rare, but interesting, plants listed as well, like Sundew, a fly-eating plant, and Death Camas, which is...deadly! There are more plants on the Coast than there is room in this book! And they are all interesting!

The many medicines of the Coastal ecosystem.

Plant Names and Language

You will notice as you read this book that when we talk about plants we use different types of names. Common names are the names English-speaking people have given to the plants. These names often show the colonial perspective that was current at the time of naming them, like Douglas Fir, for example. This is a tree that had been growing on the Coast for many thousands of years before there ever was such a person as David Douglas, who named the tree after himself. Douglas was a Scottish **botanist** who came to the Coast in the 1820s to gather samples of plants to send back to England. You will find many plants and animals with the name Douglas in either their common name or their Latin name. There are many other European men who named plants after themselves, claiming to have discovered them, when in reality, these plants had long been part of daily life for the Coastal Indigenous people.

Every plant (and animal for that matter) on the Coast already had a name when these European men came along and "discovered" and named them. There are thirty-four different Indigenous languages spoken in BC. In these languages, not only do plants have names, but sometimes there are names for each part of the plant, or for how a plant is used or eaten. I am not including the Indigenous names in this book because they are not mine to share, nor do I know many of them. It would take an encyclopedia to list them all!

Many common names of plants are descriptive, like Yellow Violet or Field Mint. Some plants have been given more than one common name, like Queen Anne's Lace, which is also called Wild Carrot. This can be confusing. Sometimes more than one plant has the same name, like the Fir trees, one of which is a "true" Fir and one of which is not. This is one of the reasons botanists use Latin names when talking about plants. Every plant has a Latin name—only one Latin name—so we can't mix them up. Latin is considered a "dead" language, meaning no country or culture speaks it, and only scholars and scientists use it. So they chose to use Latin names as an overall naming or classification system.

Douglas Fir and Douglas Maple?

What about Sophia Fir?

Usually, when people write about plants, the plant name is spelled with a lower case letter, like "dandelion." I have chosen to use upper case letters when writing about plants, as in "Dandelion." When we spell our names or the names of places, they start with capitals. By capitalizing the plant's name, I am hoping to remind you to see them not as "things," but as living individuals who are in a relationship with the world around them and who deserve respect.

Dos and Don'ts of Wildcrafting Plants

Plants and people have a long history together. Humans have always harvested plants to use for food, medicine, tools, clothing and other purposes. Today, we call this **wildcrafting**. When we harvest plants with awareness, the plants will continue to flourish in the future. Although plants can be abundant, we have to keep in mind that we are sharing them with the rest of our community: the animals and insects that rely on them for food and shelter, the ecosystem that depends on them in many invisible ways, and other people who may want to harvest them as well. People are supposed to interact with plants. *Do* gently pick a leaf of Mint and eat it. *Don't* grab all the leaves off Sword Ferns as you walk by. Treat plants with respect, and they will be there for you.

Here are some tips to help you become an **ethical** harvester:

Get to know the area where you are harvesting.
- Whose traditional territory are you on?
- How many plants are there?
- Do any animals use these plants for food?

- Does anyone else harvest plants from this place?
- Do dogs do their "business" on these plants? (*Yuck!*)
- Is there nearby traffic or business that might be polluting the area?
- How do the place and its plants change with the seasons?

Don't take more than one plant out of ten.

A general rule with common plants is not to take more than one plant out of ten. For example, if you are harvesting Stinging Nettles, observe approximately how many plants there are in the patch, and for every ten plants, pick just one plant.

Be careful with roots.

If you are harvesting roots, remember that unless the plant can regenerate by a part of the root being replanted, you are killing the whole plant by taking the root.

Think about the flowers' future.

Harvesting flowers means harvesting the future fruit of the plant. Roses turn into Rose hips, for example. **Pollinators**, like bees, butterflies and hummingbirds, need flowers for food. When harvesting flowers, keep this in mind.

Leave some seeds behind.

If you are picking a plant when it is in seed, make sure to leave some seeds scattered in the area for regeneration.

> Sometimes kids are told "Look but don't touch" in nature. But how will you learn if you don't nibble and smell and pick?

Symbols Used in This Book

Not edible, but
it won't kill you.

Edible.

Rare, so don't
pick it!

This plant has
medicinal uses.

This activity needs
an adult's help.

Poisonous, so
don't touch it!

Leave rare plants alone.

Never pick rare plants. If you are unsure if a plant is rare, don't pick it, and check local conservation guidelines.

Check in with the plants.

Go back to the spot you have harvested from as often as you can and in every season so you can see the impact your harvesting has on the plants and their ecosystems. Some plants may like to be thinned out, allowing more light in or allowing room for the patch to spread out.

Watch out for poison.

Never harvest plants near roads, under power lines or in other places **herbicides** or **pesticides** are sprayed.

Leave no trace.

Always make the site you harvest from look as if no one was there. Fill in holes, re-cover roots and replace leaves and mulch. This ensures the place can recover easily and the remaining plants will continue growing.

Thank the plants.

Some people like to say thank you or sing a song while they harvest. Some people like to leave a token of thanks. If you do this, make sure it is **compostable** and small.

Understanding Plant Families

Like people, plants have families. Every plant belongs to a family. Each family of plants has certain characteristics. For example, just as people in your family may have brown hair, plants in the Mint family have square stems. Learning about plant families can help us learn how to quickly identify plants and some of their uses.

Plant Families

Here are six common plant families to get to know.

Carrot (Apiaceae or Umbelliferae)

Although there are many edible plants in this family, like Carrots, Parsley and Cumin, some of the most poisonous plants in the world are in this family as well, so please do not gather these plants without a knowledgeable adult's help! The poisonous plants are Water Hemlock and Poison Hemlock.

The umbrella-like umbels of
the Carrot family flowers.

Common and not-so-poisonous plants in the Carrot family include Wild Carrot or Queen Anne's Lace, Sweet Cicely, Cow Parsnip, Angelica and Giant Hogweed.

Flowers in the Carrot family are white, yellow or reddish brown and grow in **umbels**, like umbrellas. Their seeds are small clusters forming large umbels that usually have a strong smell when crushed. The stems are often hairy and hollow with long and feathery leaves.

Heath or Heather (Ericaceae)

Many of the forest plants on the Coast belong to the Heather family. These include Salal, Arbutus, Manzanita, Kinnikinnick, Wintergreen, Cranberry, Copperbush, Rhododendron, Labrador Tea and the *Vaccinium* berries (Blueberry, Red and Black Huckleberry and Evergreen Blueberry).

The small, bell-shaped flowers of the Heath family are pink to white. The leaves of these plants are often thick and waxy. The Heather family often likes to grow in **acidic soil**.

Kinnikinnick.

Manzanita.

Close-up of a Heath
family flower.

Lily (Liliaceae)

Some of the Coast's most beautiful wildflowers are in the Lily family, like Camas, Fawn Lily and Chocolate Lily. There are a lot of showy garden flowers in this family, and even Asparagus and Onions are lilies! When you think of Lilies, you can think in threes. There are three petals, three **sepals** and six **stamens**, and the seed capsule has three chambers to it. The leaves of plants in the Lily family all have **parallel veins**, meaning they run side by side.

Camas flower.

Mint (Lamiaceae)

Many common kitchen herbs are in the Mint family, including Oregano, Rosemary, Thyme and Mint, of course. Some of the many wild plants in the mint family are Motherwort, Bee Balm, Stink Mint, Water Horehound, Skullcap, Yerba Buena and Field Mint.

The small flowers in the Mint family are white, pink, purple or blue and are shaped like little trumpets. The stems are square with **lance-shaped** leaves that grow **opposite** each other on the stem. All these plants smell strong, but not always "minty." They contain high amounts of **volatile oils**, which give them their scent and also mean that many of them are good for colds and flus.

Square stems of the Mint family.

Mae and the Mint.

This Rose has five petals.

Rose (Rosaceae)

Most Rose family plants make edible fruits, like Blackberries, Raspberries, Thimbleberries, Apples, Crab Apples, Pears, Strawberries, Hawthorn and Rose hips.

The sweet-smelling flowers are pink, white, yellow or red, and always have petals in multiples of five. The stems are often thorny or hairy. The leaves in the Rose family are usually opposite, lance-shaped and **serrated** (jagged).

Sunflower or Aster (Asteraceae or Compositae)

Some common wild plants in the Aster family are Yarrow, Chicory, Tansy, Hairy Cat's Ear, Oxeye Daisy, Goldenrod and of course Dandelion! Lettuce is in the Aster family too. The flowers in the Aster family are tricky! These yellow, orange, white, purple or pink flowers look like one big flower, but when you look closer, there are many, sometimes hundreds, of tiny flowers all bunched together. Some Aster flowers have outer **bracts** that look like petals but are really a kind of leaf. The rest of the "real" leaves are often hairy or soft and lance-shaped. The Aster family is the second-largest family of plants in the world, after Orchids.

A **subclass** of the Aster family is the Dandelion family. These flowers are usually yellow to orange and have straight-ended petals. The leaves on these plants are often toothed, hairy or serrated. The plants in the Dandelion subfamily are edible, but all have milky white sap in the stems that makes them bitter.

An Aster flower up close.

Plant Guilds

Plants do not often grow on their own; they like to grow with other plants. When plants commonly grow with each other, we call these **plant guilds**. You could also call them plant communities. Sometimes plants grow together because they need each other; for example, Ghost Pipe needs the roots of **coniferous** (**evergreen**) trees to help feed itself. Other plants often grow together because they like similar soil, like Evergreen Huckleberry and Salal, which both like acidic soil. Cattail, Crab Apple and Skunk Cabbage all like moist to wet soil, and so they grow together. Understanding where plants like to grow and which other plants they like to grow with can help you figure out where you might find a plant or give you more information about what this plant is like. I also like the idea of plants having "friends." Humans are the same—there are people we choose to be around because we like them. Perhaps plants grow next to other plants because they like each other too.

Camas flowers growing

under Garry Oaks.

A Coastal tree guild of Douglas Fir, Bigleaf Maple and Arbutus,

growing together on the southern tip of Denman Island.

Poisonous Plants

Getting to know plants is exciting! All of a sudden there are friends, snacks, medicines and crafts all around you. But getting to know plants really well is important, because there are some very poisonous plants that grow in our Coastal region, and many plants have look-alikes that can be hard to tell apart without practice.

An important thing to keep in mind when meeting any plant for the first time, especially poisonous ones, is to consult an adult who knows about plants before you touch them. Only eat plants you have eaten before with an adult. If you need to handle a poisonous plant for further identification, wear gloves and make sure to wash your hands well afterward. Do not put your hands on your face or in your mouth. Most poisonous plants will make you sicker the more you eat. If you ate one little tiny crumb of Death Camas, it could give you a tummy ache, but if you ate a whole bulb, you would get terribly sick and vomit and have fevers. If you ate a few bulbs, you could die. So, because you don't want any of these things to happen, be careful but curious when meeting poisonous plants.

Two of the most poisonous plants we live near are **Douglas's Water Hemlock** (*Cicuta douglasii*) and its cousin,

> Never touch or eat a plant if you don't know what it is.

Water Hemlock.

"Vein to the cut, hurts my gut!"

Poison Hemlock (*Conium maculatum*). These are both in the Carrot, or Apiaceae, family. You will find them growing in wet areas, like ditches, lakesides, marshes and ponds. There is even a patch right by our swim spot at the lake. Learning how to tell these plants apart from other plants in the Carrot family is important, because there are many other wonderful plants in the Carrot family to get to know, like Wild Carrot (*Daucus carota*), Spring Gold (*Lomatium utriculatum*) and Cow Parsnip (*Heracleum lanatum*).

A great way to identify Water Hemlock is by looking closely at the leaves. The **veins** of the leaves go to the cut in the leaf, whereas other plants in the Carrot family have leaves with the vein going to the tip of the leaf. Another way to tell this plant apart from its non-poisonous cousins is by cutting open the base of the stalk while wearing gloves. The bulging part at the base is made up of hollow chambers. One of these is enough to kill a cow! It causes **convulsions** and shuts down the **nervous system**. Holy cow!

Another important poisonous plant to know in the Coastal region is **Death Camas** (*Zigadenus venenosus*). Can

The great Greek philosopher Socrates died from drinking Water Hemlock tea.

you guess why it is called Death Camas? You don't want to eat this plant. If you do, it can make you feel really sick to your stomach, make you throw up, make it hard to breathe and finally put you into a coma! Yikes! The thing is, Death Camas often grows with its cousin, Common Camas, a very beautiful bluish-purple Lily whose bulb is an important food source for Indigenous people on the Coast. Because the bulbs of both of these plants look similar, people have to weed out the Death Camas from the Common Camas while the plants are in flower, so that when they harvest the Common Camas bulbs later in the year with the flowers gone, they can make sure they aren't accidentally harvesting Death Camas.

Death Camas.

"Will I die if I accidentally touch the leaves of the Death Camas, Philippa?" Sophia, age 11, asked me nervously as we watched a bee gather nectar from the cream-coloured flowers. "And why isn't the bee dying if it is eating the Death Camas?" "No, you won't die if you accidentally touch it," I tell her, "but give this powerful plant some space. As for the bee, get this: many insects are attracted to the Death Camas's showy flowers, but once they try to fly away they are unable to, because they have been poisoned. It is common to see a ring of dead insects around a Death Camas. There is only one pollinator that is somehow immune to the toxins in the Death Camas, and that is the Death Camas Miner Bee. This bee feeds the pollen from Death Camas to its larvae. If a **parasite** wasp tries to take over the bees' nest, it is poisoned by eating the pollen it steals." "Whoa," Sophia says, "those Death Camas Miner Bees are not only smart, but they are brave too!"

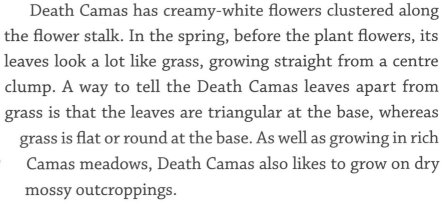

Foxglove.

Death Camas has creamy-white flowers clustered along the flower stalk. In the spring, before the plant flowers, its leaves look a lot like grass, growing straight from a centre clump. A way to tell the Death Camas leaves apart from grass is that the leaves are triangular at the base, whereas grass is flat or round at the base. As well as growing in rich Camas meadows, Death Camas also likes to grow on dry mossy outcroppings.

Foxglove (*Digitalis purpurea*) is a favourite plant of kids, who love the colourful bell-shaped flowers, and of bumble-bees, who love the pollen. It is also a poisonous Coastal plant that was first introduced from Europe. Foxglove is in the Figwort family, along with Mullein. Because the leaves look similar to other useful plants' leaves, like Comfrey and Mullein, it is important to learn what Foxglove looks like when not in flower. All three plants have large soft **basal** leaves in the first year of growth. Foxglove leaves are crinkly on the edge and thinner than Comfrey and Mullein leaves. Mullein leaves are quite thick and soft, and Comfrey leaves are straight along the edge, not toothed or crinkly. Although pick-ing the Foxglove flowers

"Being able to tell Foxglove from Mullein is important. You could get really sick if you mix them up."
—Arawyn, age 12

and putting one on every finger, like a lovely pair of gloves, won't kill you, sometimes even just touching the leaves can give you a rash. But eating any of the plant can make your heart stop working. In fact, this plant is so powerful that a medication for treating heart problems is made out of it.

Snowberry (*Symphoricarpos albus*) is called "Saskatoon Berry from the Land of the Dead" in Stl'atl'imx stories from the Interior of BC. Why? Because it is also poisonous! On the Coast, we are lucky to have many types of edible berries and only a few poisonous ones. Snowberries are the only white berry on a native bush growing on the Coast. They are in the Honeysuckle

Snowberry.

"No, Kaya! Don't eat those. They are berries from the land of the dead!"

There are only a few poisonous berries on the Coast. They are Honeysuckle (*Lonicera ciliosa*) berries, raw Red Elderberries, Yew berries and Snowberries.

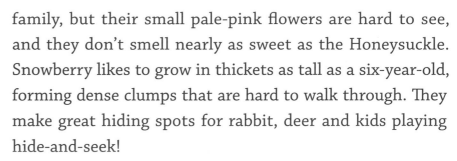

family, but their small pale-pink flowers are hard to see, and they don't smell nearly as sweet as the Honeysuckle. Snowberry likes to grow in thickets as tall as a six-year-old, forming dense clumps that are hard to walk through. They make great hiding spots for rabbit, deer and kids playing hide-and-seek!

It would be hard to live on the Coast and not know **Scotch Broom** (*Cytisus scoparius*)! Broom is a European shrub that can grow taller than an adult in dry **disturbed** sites. In June, the yellow flowers come out, making the whole landscape where they grow bright yellow. Honeybees and bumblebees love the nectar and the pollen from these flowers and can be heard buzzing among the flowers, the pollen sacs on their legs full of the golden pollen. Because Broom is in the pea family, when it is done flowering, it makes small black pea-like pods that contain small black seeds. These harmless-looking seeds are what get kids and farm animals in trouble, causing stomach upset and even a shutdown of the heart and nervous system when eaten. Many of the wild pea family plants in our region are also poisonous, so use caution when touching them.

Scotch Broom.

Invasive Plants

You may have heard the term **invasive plants** or non-native plants before. This term refers to plants that do not originate in North America. A common example on the Coast is Scotch Broom. This woody shrub was brought to Sooke, BC, outside Victoria, in 1850, by a Scottish man who wanted a plant that reminded him of home. Three seeds and many years later, Scotch Broom is one of the most prolific plants on the Coast.

A field of Scotch Broom.

A Camas meadow in full bloom with Scotch Broom slowly taking over.

Scotch Broom is neither "good" nor "bad." It is just doing the job it knows how to do.

Like most things in the world, deciding whether Scotch Broom and invasive plants in general are "good" or "bad" is a difficult question. Scotch Broom grows in open areas. This means it can take over the important and rare habitat of meadow plants like our rare Garry Oak and wildflower ecosystems. On the other hand, Scotch Broom has grown in and covers the clear-cut I live next to. It is holding together soil that might otherwise erode, has made shelter for the White-Crowned Sparrows who nest in these dense shrubs, and is offering nitrogen to the soil, which has been depleted. In an ideal situation, humans would not be clear-cutting forests, nor would they have brought these seeds in, and the plants would not be destroying fragile ecosystems.

Many of the common plants we know on the Coast are non-native. Plants strive to rebalance what is off. Most grasses we see here are non-native. Many plants that grow where the soil or **ecology** has been disturbed are non-native. Some common invasive and non-native plants are Thistle, which brings up nutrients from the soil but is prickly and takes over grazing pasture; Buttercup, which helps break up thick clumpy soil with its roots but is poisonous to animals; and Japanese Knotweed, which is a strong and important medicine for Lyme disease but forms dense thickets that shade out other plants and can even crack through concrete. These are a few examples of how it is difficult to say whether a plant is "bad" or "good."

What is the invasive plant doing? Is it providing food for birds? Is it shading out wildflowers? Is it holding in soil? Is it

> Our job as people who care for the land and know about plants is to notice how a plant is affecting where it grows.

A Camas meadow with an old Oak in behind.

causing animals to get sick? Are the roots pushing out other roots? Bluebells and Daffodils push out Camas bulbs. When we know the land and the plants, we then have an idea of how and when to help. You might concentrate your efforts on pulling Scotch Broom from the meadow where wild-flowers grow, instead of from the old clear-cut. You might see some English Ivy or Holly just beginning to take hold in your favourite woods and pull it out. But the big thicket of Blackberry might be pruned and enjoyed for the berries it feeds you and your family throughout the winter.

Plant Profiles

Here are some plants you may be likely to meet in wild areas, parks and forests on the Coast. They are arranged by season so you will know when to look for them. Within each season they are arranged alphabetically. The Latin name is in *italics* next to each common name. You'll also find some great activities to do with the plants in every season.

There are many ways to learn about plants. Use all your senses: your eyes, your hands, your ears, your nose and your mouth!

Sophia and Margret play the blindfold game.

Spring

In spring, plants begin their growth. It is a time of fresh new shoots, blossoms, flowers and edible greens. Bees are busy **pollinating** flowers. The soil is warming up enough for seeds dropped last fall to begin to sprout.

Cottonwoods in fluff.

Black Cottonwood

or Balsam Poplar

*Populus balsamifera
ssp. trichocarpa*

Guild: Osier Dogwood, Maple, Mock Orange, Alder, Douglas Fir, Horsetail

Description

Cottonwood is most easily known by the sweet smell the buds give off in the spring. These buds are full of sticky golden sap. Cottonwood is a **deciduous** tree with waxy heart-shaped leaves and big fluffy white **catkins** that give the tree its name. This tree likes to grow in moist areas like marsh and lake edges and near streams and rivers. It can grow as tall as a ten-storey building, and when it gets old, the grey bark gets deeply grooved. Cottonwood is in the same family as Willow.

Cool Facts about Cottonwood

Cottonwood is an important **wildlife tree**, which means a tree where animals like to live. When these trees get old, the bark can peel away from the trunk, making great homes for bats. The limbs blow off easily, and the resulting holes can become homes for many animals, including Pileated Woodpeckers, Northern Flickers, Western Screech Owls, Northern Saw-Whet Owls, Goldeneyes, Buffleheads, Wood

Ducks and even Black Bears. Ospreys, Great Blue Herons and Bald Eagles will often build their nests in the tops of tall Cottonwoods, giving them a great view of the waters around them for fishing. In June, when the catkins open, Cottonwood fluff floats on the breeze, sometimes making small drifts of sweet-smelling Cottonwood "snow" on the ground.

Cottonwood bud.

I once saw a family of raccoons living in the hole of a Cottonwood, the babies sticking their cute noses out, waiting for their mother to return. They were so cute I wanted to pick one up and cuddle it. But I didn't, of course. It is important not to touch wild animals.

Harvesting Tip
. . . .

It is common for branches to blow down off the Cottonwood in the big winds of winter. The easiest way to harvest the buds is from these limbs on the ground.

MAKE COTTONWOOD BUD OIL

Supplies needed:
- Cottonwood buds
- oil like olive, almond, avocado, apricot kernel or grape seed
- large glass jar
- rubbing alcohol for cleaning up

Note: The sap is very sticky, and you will need to use rubbing alcohol to clean anything that gets sappy.

Cottonwood buds might be one of the best smells on earth. In the late winter and early spring, when the buds are full of sap, I often walk around with a sticky yellow nose from smelling the sap. I promise it is not snot! It is the sap from the Cottonwood. But there are more graceful ways of smelling like Cottonwood. One way to do this is to make an oil from the buds. All you need to do is bring a bag or a jar to the Cottonwood and collect the buds by breaking them off and putting them in your jar. When you get home, cover the buds with an oil of your choice: olive oil, almond oil, grape seed oil and apricot kernel oil all work well. Cover the jar with its lid, and let the buds sit in this oil for about six weeks. After that, strain off the oil and compost the buds. You can wear the oil like perfume or make a healing and beautiful smelling salve with it by following the directions for Plantain (page 106).

Cottonwood buds to make oil.

Katrina Rainoshek

Guild: Red Cedar, Douglas Fir, Trailing Blackberry, Yerba Buena, Cascara

Bracken Fern

Pteridium aquilinum

Description

Bracken Fern can grow as tall as me! (But I am only 161 centimetres, or 5′3″.) With big feathery **fronds** that are divided into leaves on either side of the stem, this fern looks different from the other common ferns on the Coast. It likes to grow in open clearings, in meadows, on roadsides and in other sunny locations.

Cool Facts about Bracken Fern

Bracken Fern is a fast-growing deciduous Fern. It dies back in the winter, and in the spring unfurls from little green spirals. It grows so fast that, from one day to the next, you can almost see it unfurling. Bracken Fern is one of the most common ferns in the world, growing all across the **northern hemisphere**.

"Dried Bracken Fern makes a good bed when you lay them down on the ground. I like to build a nest out of them and have a nap." —Briar, age 8

Bracken fern.

Breah and Alexander measure
Bracken Fern. Katrina Rainoshek

MEASURE THIS

Supplies needed:

- notebook
- pencil
- measuring tape

Watching plants grow sounds like a boring thing to do. But not always. When you can almost see the plant grow before your eyes, you can see the magic of **photosynthesis**, or how plants "eat." In April or May, find a patch of Bracken Fern that you can visit every day, or every week. Bring a tape measure, pencil and notebook. Choose one Bracken Fern that is just coming up and measure it. Make a drawing in your notebook and record your observations. Continue to measure the Bracken Fern regularly, drawing it as it changes, and noting how quickly it grows. Here are some questions to ask: Does it grow at the same rate throughout the spring? Are there times it grows faster or slower? What helps it to grow so quickly? How long does it take to reach full size? How tall would you be if you grew this fast?

Guild: Spirea, Yellow Iris, Yellow Pond Lily, Bulrush, Cascara, Salmonberry

Description

Have you ever seen a hot dog growing on a stick in the shallow water of ponds, marshes, lakesides and ditches? Well, then you have seen Cattail. It is a tall plant, up to 2.5 metres (9 feet) tall, with long, narrow, flat, kind of spongy leaves that grow almost straight up. In the spring, Cattail sends up shoots, which then turn into a dense cluster of tiny brown flowers that form that hot dog shape. Above the brown part is a spike of light-brown pollen. Late in the summer, when Cattail goes to seed, the "hot dog" turns into white fluff that goes sailing across the water.

Cattail.

Cattail

Typha latifolia

CAUTION: When harvesting the roots and shoots, be sure not to confuse Cattail with Yellow Iris, which is poisonous and a spreading invasive plant around lakes and marshes on the Coast.

The fleshy and tasty stalk of Cattail.

Cool Facts about Cattail

What plant can be a lantern, diapers, pancakes, corn on the cob, food, a roof, a sleeping mat, medicine, a duck, clothes, ropes, dishes, pillows and a blanket?! Cattail! In her book *Braiding Sweetgrass*, Robin Wall Kimmerer calls Cattail the "Walmart of the marsh," or just "Wal-marsh," because of how many ways it can be used. The stalks can be cut at the bottom with a flowering top, and this "hot dog" can be dipped in oil to make a lantern or torch. The seed fluff was and can be used to stuff pillows, mattresses and diapers. A flour can be made from the pollen and turned into pancakes. When the seed heads are first coming out and are green, they can be steamed and eaten like corn on the cob. The roots and young shoots can be harvested, peeled and eaten. Mats, hats, capes, blankets, dishes and roof tiles can all be made by weaving cattail leaves. The goo from the stem is very soothing when applied to sunburns and rashes. Rope and twine can be made from the fibre of the leaves and stalks. And finally, a duck that floats can be made by folding Cattail leaves together. All these uses for Cattail were like Walmart for people before the days of stores.

CATTAIL DUCKS

Cut a long Cattail leaf at its base. Starting from the cut end of the leaf, fold the leaf around itself in folds as long as your hand; this forms the base of the duck. Leave enough of the end of the leaf to be folded up to become the duck's neck, then fold the tip of the leaf over to make the beak. You can tie the body of the duck together with a thin strip torn from another leaf of Cattail. Now try to float your duck on the water. You may have to adjust its balance if it tips over.

Floating Cattail duck.

Cattail duck.

Harvesting Cattail is a fun and messy job, best done on a warm day with your pants rolled up or even in a bathing suit! The roots and shoots of Cattail are quite good to eat. Cattail spreads by **rhizomes**, which are roots that run along the surface of the ground. In spring and then again in fall, these roots have shoots on them that can be snapped off, peeled and eaten raw or cooked. Be sure that you are harvesting Cattail and not Iris, which is poisonous and looks similar when it is leafing out. The white inner part of the fleshy rhizomes can be eaten the same way. To harvest the pollen to use as a protein-rich flour, place a paper bag over top of the pollen stem and shake the bag, releasing the pollen.

The kids at Salix School liked the shoots of the Cattail so much that they began fighting over them. It is best to harvest with calm gratitude; otherwise, you might end up covered head to toe in mud!

Harvesting Cattail shoots.

Zemera eats the Cattail shoot.

Guild: Miner's Lettuce

Chickweed

Stellaria media

and Miner's Lettuce
Claytonia perfoliata

Description

Chickweed is a small, spreading, low-growing plant with little heart-shaped green leaves. In early summer it grows small white flowers. Miner's Lettuce is also a small low-growing plant, but it clumps rather than spreads. The spade-shaped leaves are larger than Chickweed's and more fleshy. When the plant gets older, the leaves form a circle around the stalk, which sends up a little star-shaped flower.

Both of these plants like to grow where there is some moisture in the ground, like at the base of Oak trees, in lush garden beds and at edges of woods.

Cool Facts about Chickweed and Miner's Lettuce

Both of these plants are edible and delicious early in the spring. They are yummy eaten as a snack when you're out and about, or picked to make an early spring salad. I have picked them as early as January, when there is not much else fresh to eat.

Chickweed and Miner's Lettuce.

When these plants go to flower, they start to get too strong to eat and can cause an uncomfortable feeling in the back of your throat. One day in late spring, Rueben, age 9, saw a lush patch of Miner's Lettuce and grabbed a whole handful, pulling them out by the roots, and gobbled them up. "Yuck!" he shouted, as he spat them out. "They make my throat feel like it is full of nails." This was a little reminder from the plants to harvest them with care.

Because both of these plants have lots of water in them, they are soothing when applied to burns and sunburns, rashes like eczema and Nettle stings. Just chew them up and put them on the place that hurts.

EARLY WILD SALAD

Head out into the wild grocery store to see what you can make into a salad. February and March are great times to find all kinds of wild greens to eat. Try Chickweed, Miner's Lettuce, Dandelion greens, Dandelion flowers, a few Red Flowering Currant flowers, Maple blossoms, Sheep Sorrel leaves, Fir needle tips, young Curly Dock leaves or Salmonberry flowers and shoots. What could be better than a salad you harvest yourself from the generous free grocery store of the outdoors? Just make sure you pick these plants gently and away from where dogs pee or cars drive.

Supplies needed:
- wild greens
- bowl
- scissors

Collecting a wild salad.

Katrina Rainoshek

Chocolate Lily

Fritillaria lanceolata

Guild: Death Camas, Fawn Lily, Garry Oak, Camas, Saskatoon Berry, Arbutus

Description

Chocolate Lily likes to grow in warm meadows; on rocky outcroppings of ridges, hills and boulders; and in moist meadows with its Lily cousins. As a **perennial**, Chocolate Lily is a plant that grows from the same bulb year after year, adding new flowers as it grows. The dark-brown colour of its petals gives this Lily its name, although it is also checkered with yellow squares like a chess board, giving it its other name, Checkered Lily. The dainty flowers droop down, but when they go to seed, the pods turn up to show you their small black seeds. The leaves of the Chocolate Lily grow in a **whorl**, each lance-shaped leaf coming off the stem in a circle.

Chocolate lily.

These plants can take seven years to make one flower. When I saw a Chocolate Lily with seven flowers once on Hornby Island, I knew the plant could have been almost fifty years old!

There is a place near the beach where Chocolate Lily grows so thick that I have to tiptoe through it to get to the Cottonwood trees in behind when I go harvest the buds. Like many places up and down the Coast, this was probably once someone's garden, tended and cared for by the Indigenous families who lived here before the settlers came.

Gathering Chocolate Lily seeds.

Cool Facts about Chocolate Lily

Like the other wild Lilies of the Coast, Chocolate Lily is quite rare and should just be admired where it grows. These Lilies bloom around Easter, and sometimes I like to tell kids that the Easter Bunny has come and left them some chocolate! (It doesn't taste like chocolate, but it sure is pretty.) Northern Rice Root, a cousin of Chocolate Lily, looks similar, except the brown flowers are bunched at the top of the plant, and it prefers to grow in **estuaries** with Silverweed and Cow Parsnip. Both plants have roots that are traditionally harvested for food by Indigenous people up and down the Coast.

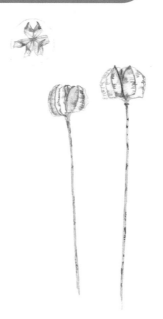

Chocolate Lily seed pods.

Chocolate Lily   47

Dandelion

Taraxacum officinale

Dandelion.

Guild: Plantain; lawns, gardens

Description

Dandelion is in the Aster family. Although many people think they know a Dandelion when they see one, this plant has many look-alikes, because the Aster family is so big. Hairy Cat's Ear (*Hypochaeris radicata*) looks a lot like Dandelion. Learning to tell the two apart is important, because one is good to eat and the other...not so good! (Plus, you can impress people by telling them apart!)

Dandelion differs from Hairy Cat's Ear by having smooth stems and leaves, with the leaves having sharp hooked "teeth." The yellow petals of Dandelion are flat on the ends. Dandelion tends to flower in the spring and then again in the fall, whereas Hairy Cat's Ear can flower throughout the summer. Hairy Cat's Ear has **lobed**, toothed, slightly fuzzy leaves and stems, and can produce multiple flowers from one stem, which is usually slimmer than a Dandelion's stem. Dandelions make great puffy seed heads that are good for making wishes on, whereas the Hairy Cat's Ear won't grant any wishes—the seeds stay bunched together when they are blown. Both of these plants have a white milky liquid in their stems.

Cool Facts about Dandelion

Dandelions are originally from Europe and were first brought to North America as a food plant. The leaves are edible (but not the leaves of Hairy Cat's Ear, which are tough and bitter) and are best eaten when they are young, in the spring before they flower. You can just pick them and munch them as a snack or add them to salads. The flowers are also edible and look pretty sprinkled in a salad.

Dandelions are very good for you as well, full of iron, potassium, calcium and vitamins A, B, C and E. You could just eat some Dandelion leaves instead of taking your vitamins. Some people find Dandelion bitter, but this bitter quality is actually part of the medicine, helping your body clean the blood by supporting your liver. The white sap in the stem of Dandelion makes warts go away if you put it on the wart three times a day.

Dandelion gets its name from *dent-de-lion*, meaning "tooth of the lion" in French, due to the sharp teeth of the leaves. It is also known as *pis-en-lit* in French, which means "to pee the bed," because Dandelion leaves can make you pee if you eat a lot.

Hairy Cat's Ear.

Be careful when making a wish on Dandelion seeds. The seeds can blow into your eyes, and they are hard to get out!

Dandelion seeds can travel up to 100 kilometres (62 miles) on the wind.

MAKE YOUR OWN KIDS' COFFEE

Supplies needed:
- Dandelion roots
- small shovel or garden trowel
- baking tray
- kitchen knife
- coffee grinder
- oven
- cream and honey (optional)

Isabella drinks her Dandelion coffee.

Katrina Rainoshek

Isabella makes Dandelion coffee.

Katrina Rainoshek

Have you ever tried a sip of an adult's coffee? Did you like it? If so, now you can make your own, without all the caffeine! Lots of people don't know how great Dandelions are and wish they wouldn't grow in their lawn or garden. You can offer a Dandelion root-weeding service. Use an old butter knife or hand trowel to dig up the roots. When you have at least a handful of roots, wash them, then chop them up small (if you need help with a knife, ask an adult). Spread the roots out on a baking tray and roast them in the oven at 350°F for about twenty minutes. Have an adult help you with the hot oven and pan. Once the roots are roasted and cooled, you can grind them up in a coffee grinder. To make the "coffee," boil 1 cup of water and simmer 1 heaping teaspoon of the roots for ten minutes. Strain and add cream and honey to taste. Yum—your very own "coffee"!

Guild: Garry Oak, Licorice Fern, Arbutus, Alder

Description

Fawn Lilies are so pretty, with their six white petals that swoosh back from the stem as they nod their heads over. The flowers come out in April among Licorice Ferns atop mossy rocks or on the sunny side of moist banks. Once in a while you will be lucky to find a Pink Fawn Lily (*Erythronium revolutum*) growing among the white ones, or a Yellow Glacier Lily (*Erythronium grandiflorum*), which grows up high in the mountains with yellow flowers. The leaves of the plant are what gave it the name Fawn Lily, as their mottled-brown-and-red colour looks similar to the speckled coat of a baby deer. Don't pick these plants—like the rest of their wild Lily cousins, they are quite rare.

"Fawn Lilies look like cool dude flowers. I could even see them wearing sunglasses."
—Breah, age 9

Fawn Lily

Erythronium oregonum

Fawn Lily.

Camas, White Fawn Lily and Chocolate Lily are easily spread by seed.

Fawn Lily seed head.

Hawthorn flower.

Guild: Crab Apple, Rose, Osier Dogwood

Hawthorn

Black Hawthorn

Crataegus douglasii

Common Hawthorn

Crataegus monogyna

Description

Hawthorn is a small deciduous tree in the Rose family with scaly bark that likes to grow in clearings, at roadsides and in hedgerows. Its leaves are small and **lobed** and can resemble the leaves of Crab Apple. When the Hawthorn flowers in May, it is a wonderful cloud of small white blooms with pink-and-yellow centres that smell sweet and attract many bees. Like plants in the Rose family, there are five petals on each flower and five seeds in each berry. The Black Hawthorn is our native Hawthorn, which makes blue-black berries that are a little plumper than those of the

Nibble This!

Hawthorn berries are yummy to nibble on. They are like little Apples, but a bit mealy.

Hawthorn berry.

Common Hawthorn, its European cousin with smaller red berries. Both trees can have long pointy thorns, but not all trees do.

Cool Facts about Hawthorn

There are 280 different species of Hawthorn in the world. In Europe it is sometimes called the May Tree for the time of year it blooms. Hawthorn has long been thought of as a faerie tree, and it was said that a twig from a Hawthorn above the door would keep bad faeries away. Hawthorn makes a strong medicine for the heart, and it helps heal broken hearts. This may be true for people, but you will be unlucky if you are a small bird, a dragonfly or a mouse caught by a bird called a Northern Shrike. This bird uses the thorns of the Hawthorn to impale its prey before it eats it! On the Coast, the dense wood of the Hawthorn is useful for making tools, and the berries can be eaten but are not delicious.

A Northern Shrike with a mouse impaled on a Hawthorn spike. Yakubovich Dmitry

Hawthorn   53

Akai sits with a Hawthorn tree.

Try This!

. . . .

SITTING WITH HAWTHORN

Some people believe plants can "talk." "Some people" includes me. If we agree plants are alive, then surely we must be able to communicate with them somehow. In Indigenous cultures all over the world, people have learned, and continue to learn, about the uses of plants from the plants themselves. Now it's your turn. Try this.

Choose a tree that you like. There doesn't have to be any reason you like it; you can just feel drawn to it. Now, without any distractions—no books or pen, no screen or friends to talk to— find a place to sit near the tree (without getting thorns in your pants). Sit quietly for a while. Trees can take a while to say what they are thinking. You can introduce yourself, and you can ask a question, either out loud or in your head. Pay attention to how your body feels. How does your breath feel? Do any pictures come into your mind?

It's okay if you don't have any special experience, but you might notice you feel more at ease, calmer and happier. This is an especially great thing to do if you are feeling sad or lonely, and it can be done with any plant or tree, anytime, anywhere. The more you do it, the better you get at trusting what the plant is telling you and at being quiet and still.

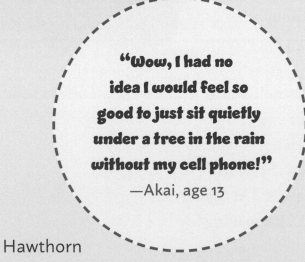

"Wow, I had no idea I would feel so good to just sit quietly under a tree in the rain without my cell phone!"
—Akai, age 13

Guild: Skunk Cabbage, Bulrush, Alder, marsh grasses; garden beds

Horsetail

Equisetum arvense

Description

Horsetail grows in two ways. The **sterile** plant does not make **spores** to reproduce. It is green, with the fringe of what looks like needles growing outward from the segments of the hollow stalk. When the plant is young, the needles are folded inward, and as it grows, they open downward. The other growth is the **fertile** plant, which makes spores for reproduction. It is creamy whitish-brown, with no needles, but a funny cone shape on top. Both versions of Horsetail grow in spreading clumps separate from each other in rich, wet, marshy ground.

Another name for Horsetail is Scouring Rush, because it is good for scrubbing and polishing things. I have used it for cleaning dishes when camping, as a toothbrush if I forget one and to polish wood after carving.

The Latin name for Horsetail, *Equisetum*, comes from the Latin name for "horse," which is *equus*.

Cool Facts about Horsetail

Horsetail plants are one of the oldest plants in the world! They were on earth 100 million years ago (a mind-boggling number), when the first animals crawled out of the sea. Horsetails at this time were as tall as an old-growth Fir tree! Somehow these plants survived the great extinction at the end of the Paleozoic period, when 95 percent of life on the planet was wiped out. They are not nearly as tall now, but they are still pretty amazing plants. They are actually more like ferns, in that they reproduce by sending out spores instead of using seeds, like other plants.

Horsetail contains a lot of a mineral called silica, which is what makes it scrubby and is also what makes up a lot of our hair, teeth and nails. Some people drink a tea made from Horsetail to strengthen their nails.

> Kids call Horsetail "Lego plant" because you can pull apart the stem and then stick it back together.

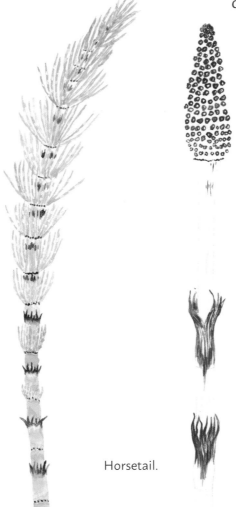

Horsetail.

USE YOUR MEMORY

One person collects some things from nature—the top of a Horsetail plant, a Hemlock cone, three different leaves, a cool stone or whatever else catches their eye. Anywhere between five and ten pieces works, depending on the age of the players. The collector then arranges these items on a bandana and covers it with a second bandana. The players gather around the bandana, and the collector tells them how long they have to look at the items arranged beneath. Ten to thirty seconds usually works. Once their time is up, they have to go out and find all the items and arrange them in the same order on their own bandanas. The collector can be generous and give the players another peek. When all players have had a chance to get their arrangements as close as possible to the collector's, lift up the bandanas so the players can see what they got right and what they have missed.

Variations: Once the players have their items arranged, give each player a turn to talk about one of their items. Or keep challenging the players' memories by rearranging the items while the players close their eyes, and then having the players try to spot what has been moved. You can play with themes like leaves, flowers or cones, too.

Supplies needed:

- two bandanas or other pieces of cloth for each player

The memory game.

Horsetail   **57**

Nootka Rose.

Rose

Baldhip Rose or Dwarf Rose

Rosa gymnocarpa

Nootka Rose

Rosa nutkana

Guild:
Blackberry,
Crab Apple,
Snowberry, Douglas Fir

"Wild Roses are beautiful, and you can eat them!"
—Beckett, age 11

Description

There are two main kinds of Rose on the Coast. There is the Baldhip Rose, or Dwarf Rose, whose flowers are the size of a quarter and have oval-shaped hips the size of your thumb. The thorns on the Baldhip Rose are very small and thin, more like slivers than thorns. The Nootka Rose, which is bigger, has flowers that are light to very dark pink and round hips the size of a gumball. The leaves of both of these Roses are oval and sharply **serrated**. All plants in the Rose family have alternate leaves and are deciduous. In the winter, these wild

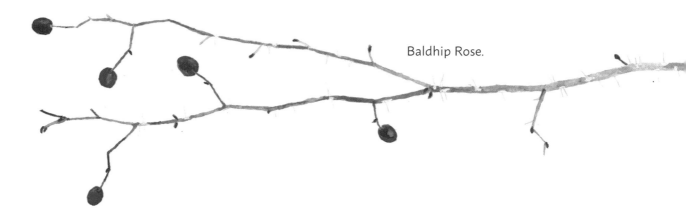
Baldhip Rose.

Roses have striking red stems. Roses like to grow in ditches, in moist places where they get some sun, at forest edges and in clearings.

Cool Facts about Wild Rose

Many of the fruits we eat are from the Rose family. This includes Strawberries, Apples, Pears, Plums, Peaches, Blackberries and Raspberries. The hips of wild Roses can be eaten or made into tea. One way to tell garden Roses from wild Roses is to look at their thorns. Those of the garden Roses are usually bigger and hooked.

All Rose family plants are edible.

Rose hips.

Nootka Rose hips.

MAKE YOUR OWN ROSE-PETAL HONEY

Supplies needed:

- Rose petals
- glass jar
- honey
- small pot
- strainer

In May, the air around roadside ditches, where the thickets of Roses grow, smells sweet with the fragrance of both the flowers and the leaves. Making Rose-petal honey is a way to capture the taste of late spring and eat it in the middle of winter. All you need to do is go out and harvest Rose petals. Gently tug them from the flower, being on the lookout for bees at work pollinating. Make sure you leave enough flowers for the bees to enjoy. When you have collected a few big handfuls of petals, bring them home and lay them out in a basket or on a clean cloth for a day so that they can wilt. This releases the water in them so that when you add the honey, it won't ferment or go bad.

Put the Rose petals in a jar and cover them with honey. You will need to stir the petals around in the jar to make sure the honey is mixed in. Now let this jar sit on the windowsill for at least a month. Or you can leave it all the way until November, so when you open it, the scent of spring fills your winter day.

> **"I felt like I was making food for a faerie feast when I made Rose-petal honey."**
> —Louisena, age 14

To separate the petals from the honey, place the jar with its lid on in a pot of water on the stove. Turn the heat to medium. When the water heats up, turn the stove down to low until the honey has liquified and can be strained off the Rose petals into a clean new jar. The leftover petals are delicious in desserts, on top of ice cream or stirred into tea. Yum!

Above left: Louisena makes Rose-petal honey.
Katrina Rainoshek

Above right: Rose-petal honey.
Katrina Rainoshek

The hips of the Rose, which are the fruits, are best harvested after the first frost. The cold makes the vitamin C in the Rose hips more available. Dry the hips in a basket and add them to winter teas.

Note: The hairs that surround the seeds inside the hips of the Nootka Rose can cause an itchy bum on their way out. In some Coastal Indigenous languages, this plant is called Itchy Bum! So although the Rose hips are great to nibble the fruit off of, don't eat the whole hip. They will be fine whole in tea.

Astrid and Louisena collect Nootka Rose petals for Rose-petal honey.

Katrina Rainoshek

Salmonberry flowers.

Guild: Sword Fern, Red Cedar, Douglas Fir, Salal, Red Huckleberry

Salmonberry

Rubus spectabilis

Salmonberries can be anywhere from deep ruby red to dark orange or pale peach. Try the different colours and see which one is your favourite!

Description

Salmonberry likes to grow where there is some moisture and sun in the forest. It is a common shrub at the edges of Fir forests and marshes. The light-brown stems and trunks have small prickles on them, but not the kind that hurt much. Like Thimbleberry and Blackberry, Salmonberry is deciduous and has alternate sharply toothed leaves, often in groups of three. The Salmonberry flowers are a deep-pink colour with five petals. Because the flowers come out early, the berries are also early and can be ripe as soon as late May, making them the first fresh fruit to eat after a long winter.

Cool Facts about Salmonberry

The ripening of the first Salmonberry takes place at the same time the Swainson's Thrush returns to the Coast from wintering in Mexico. This Robin-sized bird has a drab-brown back and light-orange-speckled breast. But it makes up for its drab outfit by singing an enchanting song. The notes of this song spiral up through the spring air from the cool green woods. All up and down the Coast, people have called the Swainson's Thrush the Salmonberry Bird, because its job is to ripen the Salmonberries for us to eat. And indeed, you

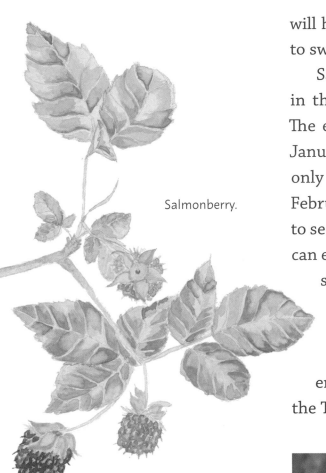
Salmonberry.

will hear the Swainson's Thrush singing the Salmonberries to sweetness too, when you listen for its rising song.

Salmonberries are one of the first flowers to come out in the spring. Sometimes they even come out in winter. The earliest we have seen these dark-pink blossoms was January 21. *Brrrrr*. In many years, the blossoms come out only to have to go back into hiding again when the snows of February come. Have a contest with your friends or family to see who can spot the first open Salmonberry flower. Who can eat the first ripe berry? The prize...the first taste of wild sweetness! One year, I promised to make a Salmonberry pie for the first kid to see a flower. Akai saw the flowers first that year but was disappointed, because by the time the Salmonberries ripened, there weren't enough Salmonberries for a pie, because the Robins and the Towhees had eaten them all!

I spy the first Salmonberry flower!
Katrina Rainoshek

Harvesting Tip

Salmonberries are soft and don't do well with being mushed in a bucket. You can put only a few at a time into a bucket or risk ending up with Salmonberry mush. They are really best eaten off the bush. In some areas, the Robins and the Towhees also love to just eat them off the bush and will eat them all! Maybe there is one you are eyeing up, waiting until it is perfectly ripe (because they really are way better ripe!), and the next day you go to eat it...and it's gone! Maybe it was your little sister...or maybe it was the Towhees.

The best berries grow at the top of the bush, just where you can't reach them, even on tiptoe. This is a good time for teamwork. My daughter likes to climb on my shoulders to reach the juicy ones right at the top.

Salmonberry feast.

Salmonberry   **65**

Skunk Cabbage

Lysichiton americanus

Guild: Horsetail, Cascara, Cattail, Alder, Salmonberry, marsh sedges

Description

You might smell Skunk Cabbage before you see it. In the spring, when Skunk Cabbage sends up its brilliant yellow flames of flowers, it also sends out its smell. I love the smell of a marsh full of Skunk Cabbage, but not everyone does. Perhaps I like it because it signals spring, as Skunk Cabbage is one of the first flowers to come out in spring, even before its leaves do. The flowers look like large yellow candle flames, but technically, those are the bracts of the flower, and the actual flowers are arranged along the spike, often covered in yellow pollen. The shiny, waxy leaves will be small in the spring, growing larger until summertime, when some of the leaves get so long they are the size of a small

Skunk Cabbage.

The whole Skunk Cabbage plant contains little crystals almost like fibreglass that can be hard on your stomach.

child! Skunk Cabbage likes to grow in marshes, ditches, muddy stream beds and **bogs**.

Cool Facts about Skunk Cabbage

Even though Skunk Cabbage can be eaten, and has been eaten in the past when there was nothing else to eat, it is better not to. I do use the roots of Skunk Cabbage in cough medicine. Check out these roots—they look like an alien from outer space! The large, smooth waxy leaves were helpful for all kinds of "kitchen" uses in the days before stores. They can be used as plates, as food wrap, for drying berries on, for layering food on in pit cooks, for lining baskets and for folding into cups. Deer love to eat Skunk Cabbage root tops, and if you walk through a marsh or muddy stream bed in the fall, you will see curious holes where the deer have dug for the roots.

Skunk Cabbage roots look like an alien from outer space!

MARSH WANDER

People often stay out of marshes. They are wet, mucky, squishy and muddy. But what could be better? Take off your shoes and socks, and leave them at the edge. Come explore. Step carefully between the giant Skunk Cabbage leaves and move silently through the Horsetail. You might see the bright jewel of a Pacific Tree Frog or come upon the smoothed-down grasses of a deer's bed. Enjoy the coolness of the mud on your feet and the melodic song of a Marsh Wren.

Enjoying the Cattails on our marsh wander.

Guild: Red Alder, Bigleaf Maple, Sword Fern, Red Huckleberry

Stinging Nettle

Urtica dioica

Description

When Nettles come up in early spring, sometimes as early as January, they are fuzzy, and sometimes almost purple. As they grow, their opposite lance- to heart-shaped leaves get less fuzzy but are still sharply toothed and covered with fine hairs. They go to flower in May, making strange little clusters of greenish-brown balls that don't really look like flowers. These turn into light-brown droops of seed clusters in the summer. Eventually, the Nettles grow so tall, up to 3 metres (9 feet), that they droop over in graceful arches, with just a few leaves and seeds clinging to the stem. The stem of Nettle is square, but don't let this confuse you: it isn't in the mint family. Nettle likes to grow in big patches in moist fields and clearings, under the dappled light of Alders and Bigleaf Maples.

Stinging Nettle.

What is cute, fuzzy and green when it is young, stings like a hundred red ants when it is middle-aged and curves gracefully like a dancer when it is old? Stinging Nettle, of course!

Sophia harvests Stinging Nettle.

Katrina Rainoshek

The sting from Nettles is made up of formic acid, the same thing that ants have in their sting!

Cool Facts about Stinging Nettle

Even though Nettles sting, they are a superfood! They are packed with protein, calcium, magnesium, vitamin C and loads of other good things. The fibre from the stalks of Nettle is very strong and has been used by Coastal Indigenous people for making rope and twine. Huge nets would be made from the Nettle fibre for fishing and catching ducks.

"If you harvest Nettles without paying attention, they will get mad at you and sting you. But if you are careful, you can harvest a lot and you won't fall in."

—Rueben, age 8

Harvesting Tip

Are you brave enough to eat Stinging Nettles? Well, here is a secret. They are delicious. And when the Nettles are cooked, blended or crushed, the stingers stop stinging. Harvest Nettle tops between late January and late April. Wear gloves if you must, but if you move slowly and carefully, you really don't need gloves. The stinging hairs are mostly on the underside of the leaves. With a pair of scissors or your knife, cut the Nettles three leaf **nodes** down, so that you are just taking the top three sets of leaves. Once you have a full bag, you can cut them up (now it's nice to wear gloves or oven mitts) and use them like spinach, but better. I like to make Nettle spanakopita, add them to omelettes or quiche, put them in smoothies, blend them into soups and even add them to muffins. I also lay fresh Nettles out to dry in baskets or dry them in a food dehydrator and keep them to make a rich nutritious tea all year. The seeds, when they are green and ripe, are a yummy, nutty-tasting snack, though sometimes they sting just a little.

Supplies needed:
- Stinging Nettle tops
- scissors
- basket or bag
- gloves

"Nettle makes good soup, and I love eating them."
—Skye, age 11

"We even put it in pancakes, and it's sooo good."
—Armas, age 9

NETTLE-SPANAKOPITA GRILLED CHEESE SANDWICHES

Ingredients:

- 1 tablespoon softened butter
- 4 slices good-quality whole-grain bread
- 1 clove garlic, sliced thin
- 2 tablespoons olive oil
- 2 big handfuls chopped Nettle leaves
- pinch each salt and freshly cracked pepper
- 1 teaspoon chopped dill
- 2 ounces feta, crumbled
- 4 thin slices cheese, such as cheddar or Havarti

Directions:

1. Either plug in a panini press or heat a skillet over medium heat. Spread butter thinly on one side of each slice of bread.

2. In a medium skillet, heat olive oil over medium-high heat, add the garlic and cook for four minutes or until the garlic is golden-brown. Add Nettles and salt and pepper, and cook for a few minutes, until the Nettles are wilted and most of the moisture is cooked out. Add dill and feta, turn off the heat and mix.

3. Assemble the sandwiches by placing two slices of bread butter side down on your press or pan. Add one slice of cheese to each, then divide the Nettle mixture in half and place half on each slice. Top with the remaining two slices of cheese and slices of bread, butter side up.

4. If using a panini press, put the lid down and cook for about five minutes, or until golden and bubbly. If using a pan, flip after about five minutes, then cook on the other side for three minutes. Goes well with a mug of Dandelion coffee (page 50).

Adobe Stock, Walid

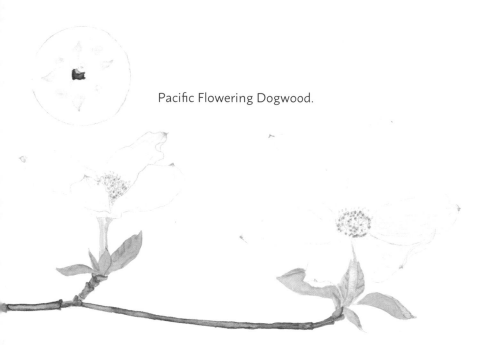
Pacific Flowering Dogwood.

Pacific Flowering Dogwood

Cornus nuttallii

Guild: Douglas Fir, Maple, Oregon Grape, Arbutus

Description

The Dogwood is a small, graceful deciduous tree whose branches remind me of a ballet dancer. Its smooth grey bark looks similar to young Maple and Cascara. The opposite lance-shaped leaves are thin and papery, turning a light red in the fall. Clusters of red berry-like fruits are ripe in the fall as well. Dogwood is most noticeable when its big white flowers appear in June. It likes to grow in rocky soil, on hillsides and in open disturbed sites.

Cool Facts about Dogwood

Although the Dogwood looks like it has big white flowers, its white petals are actually called bracts. If you look closely

Spring   73

at the centre of the "flower," you will see that the flower is actually a cluster of tiny greenish-white flowers surrounded by the large white bracts. In the olden days, its wood was used to make piano keys and sewing thread spindles.

Dogwood is the official tree of British Columbia, and it is against the law to cut it down or pick it. When I was a kid, my sister picked a flower because she thought it was pretty. I was so worried she would go to jail!

A Dogwood tree in flower.

Pacific Flowering Dogwood

Guild: Sword Fern, Alder, Douglas Fir, Salmonberry, Devil's Club

Wild Ginger

Asarum caudatum

Description

Wild Ginger grows close to the ground, with many stems forming large mats of slightly fuzzy heart-shaped leaves. The flowers come out in early spring and are a red-brown colour. They are often tucked in behind the leaves but are worth looking for because they are quite unusual, with three long squiggly petals. Wild Ginger likes to grow in moist, rich soil, often in the fallen leaves of deciduous trees, like Alder or Birch.

Wild Ginger.

Cool Facts about Wild Ginger

Aside from looking like flowers from outer space, the flowers are also interesting because they are pollinated by flies and ants, rather than by bees! The flowers smell and look like rotten meat so that flies are attracted to them and pollinate them. But don't worry, the roots don't taste like rotten meat! As its name suggests, Wild Ginger roots taste kind of like the ginger you can buy at the grocery store. In the fall or spring, you can carefully dig up a root and use it to make yummy tea that is good for stomach aches or colds. It isn't quite as spicy as regular Ginger, but it can still be used in place of it in cooking.

Ants carry the tiny black seeds of Wild Ginger around, accidentally planting them as they go. I often find large patches of Wild Ginger around ant hills.

What other plants bloom in early spring? Can you think of one more that is also stinky and pollinated by flies? (Hint: You don't want to eat this kind of cabbage!)

Too Much Ginger!

Many years ago, I was camping in the mountains north of Vancouver with a bunch of friends. Somehow we hadn't packed enough food for our week out in the woods. By the last three days, we were down to brown rice and oats. We thought we would spice up our plain food by adding some Wild Ginger to the rice while it cooked. This turned out pretty well, so the next morning, we also added Wild Ginger to our oatmeal. And then again to our rice for lunch. Well, after three days of eating Wild Ginger–flavoured everything, I couldn't wait to eat a hamburger. Nor could I bear to even think about Wild Ginger, let alone eat it again, for a long, long time!

Harvesting Tip

. . . .

Only harvest Wild Ginger from a large, healthy patch. Take no more than one root per twenty plants. Gently pull aside the top layer of soil to expose the roots, and then cut three inches of root between two nodes, so that the part left behind will continue to grow. Be sure to cover the roots back up with the soil you moved.

NATURAL VALENTINE'S DAY CARD

For a natural twist on Valentine's Day cards, pick one leaf from a healthy patch and take it home. You can trace its outline for a nice heart to make Wild Ginger valentines.

Making a Wild Ginger valentine.

Katrina Rainoshek

PLANT TAG

This is a fun way to learn the names of plants. This game can be played almost anywhere outside, from a school field to a thick forest. The person who is "it" stands in the middle of a specific area and calls out the name of a plant, shrub or tree growing nearby. Everyone else stands at the edge of the given

Playing plant tag.

"Safe!" with Wild Ginger.

area and has to run to the plant that is called without being tagged by the person who is "it." The runners are safe once they are (gently) touching the plant. If a runner is tagged, they join the "it" person in the middle; the game is over when everyone is caught.

Plant tag is great for all levels of learners, with the obvious plants, like trees, being easy to identify, and smaller green or dried-up plants, like Oxeye Daisy in the winter, being harder. People will follow the person who knows the plant being called, thereby teaching each other. This game can be played using Latin names or by describing the plant.

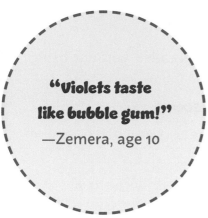

"Violets taste like bubble gum!"
—Zemera, age 10

Yellow Wood Violet

Viola glabella

Guild: Woodland Strawberry, Trailing Blackberry, Twinflower, Bracken Fern

Description

The Yellow Wood Violet is, of course, yellow, but there are other local species of Violet that are white and...violet! These small plants have flat flowers with five petals. Their leaves are generally heart-shaped and can be mistaken for Wild Ginger, whose leaves are shinier and more pointed at the end. The rare Yellow Montane Violet, which grows in Garry Oak meadows, has long egg-shaped leaves.

Cool Facts about Violets

Some bakers will coat Violets in sugar to decorate a cake. The flowers of the Violet are cool because the lower petal has stripes on it that act like a landing pad for bumblebees and butterflies, encouraging them to collect nectar from the flowers. The flower is designed so that when the bees land, they knock against the pollen and then carry the pollen to the next flower they visit, thus making sure the flowers get pollinated.

All thirteen species of Violet on the Coast are edible, though it's best not to eat rare ones.

Yellow Wood Violet.

Spring   **79**

UP CLOSE AND PERSONAL

Astrud looks at the world up close.

Supplies needed:

- note pad
- pencil
- magnifying glass

For this activity, you'll need a notepad and a pencil, and a magnifying glass if you have one. There is so much to see right in front of us that we often miss things as we walk around. Even from five feet up, I miss a lot. Get right down on your belly to see the world of the small. Choose a spot of your liking; it can be a meadow, a lawn, a thick forest, the oceanside or even a crack in the pavement. With sticks or string, square off a space about twelve inches by twelve inches. This is now your universe. Begin your exploration on the surface. Notice how many plants grow there, and if you can see any bugs or insects. Are there any signs of mammal life? Make notes in your book. Sketch what you see. Now look closer. Dig down into the soil or sand, making a little opening so you can see the world that is usually hidden to us. What is the soil like? Is it sand, clay, or rich earth? Are there bits of broken shell in it? What tiny creatures live below the surface? Spend a good quiet twenty minutes here in this little but vast universe. When you get up, the rest of the world will never look the same.

Spring Scavenger Hunt

1. Find the sign of one creature who lives where you are.
2. Collect four plants that are edible, and show them to a knowledgeable adult before you eat them.
3. Find a yellow flower, a white flower and a purple or pink flower.
4. Listen to a bird call, then go imitate it for your adult or friend.
5. Collect five different leaves that have just started growing.
6. With your finger, dig a little hole in the ground. Can you see any bugs?
7. Can you find a Fern uncurling? What kind is it?
8. What insects can you see or hear? Are they collecting pollen or nectar from a nearby flower?
9. Smell three flowers. Which one smells the sweetest?

You never know what you will find on a spring scavenger hunt.

Summer

Summer is a time of long days and heat, which brings more flowers and ripens fruit and seeds. It is a season of yummy berries to eat and long days playing outside.

Harvesting Fireweed for tea.

Trailing Blackberry.

Blackberry

Himalayan Blackberry
Rubus discolor

Evergreen Blackberry
Rubus laciniatus

Trailing Blackberry
Rubus ursinus

Guild: Meadows, clearings, ditches, roadsides and dry open woods

Description

Blackberries are hard to miss. In some places they seem to grow almost anywhere you find a bit of moisture or soil disturbance. Their thorny stems sprawl or climb in big clusters. Leaves of all species are evergreen. Himalayan Blackberry leaves are round and pointy on the end, while Evergreen Blackberry leaves look like jagged teeth. Trailing Blackberry, our only native Blackberry, is much smaller than the other two varieties. The leaves are lance-shaped, with thorns on the undersides. These have long sprawling stems that are easy to trip over as you walk through clearings in the woods where they grow. In midsummer, there are many white to pink flowers. In late summer, berries form, red at first, then

Berries in the *Rubus* clan include Blackberries, Trailing Blackberries, Blackcap Raspberries, Raspberries, Thimbleberries and Salmonberries. What similarities do you see between the plants? What differences?

ripening to black with purple juice. Blackberries are in the Rose family.

Cool Facts about Blackberries

The first two species of Blackberry are originally from Asia, but they have made themselves at home in North America for a long time. They can spread rapidly either by growing roots at the tips of their stems and rooting into the ground or by growing from seed, often dropped by birds who have eaten the berries and then pooped them out. The thick hedges they form can cause habitat loss for more sensitive plants. I have to rescue Fawn Lilies every year from the smothering vines of the Blackberry. On the other hand, these thickets provide great hiding places for rabbits, rodents and small birds. Bees love the flowers, and much honey is made from their nectar.

Trailing Blackberry plants are either female or male, and because the male plants don't make fruit, it is common to find whole patches of Trailing Blackberries without any fruit. This can be disappointing, because although these berries are not as big as their introduced cousins, they have a sweet, complex flavour that makes them one of the yummiest wild berries.

Blackberries are a delicious treat in late summer, usually ripe between mid-July and late August. They can be easily picked to make jams and pies or frozen

Himalayan Blackberry flower.

for a sweet treat in winter desserts. Not only are the berries yummy, but they are also good for you! They are the richest plant source of vitamin C and are also very high in iron. The roots of Blackberries can be used to make a good tea for diarrhea, and the leaves make a nice tea for upset tummies. So if you eat too many berries, the roots or leaves can help!

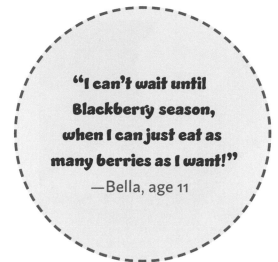

"I can't wait until Blackberry season, when I can just eat as many berries as I want!"
—Bella, age 11

Trailing Blackberry.

Blackberry jam.

To make an easy berry-picking bucket, get an old yogourt container and poke two holes across from each other at the top. Tie a length of string through so it can hang around your neck. That way you can pick twice as fast, because you can use both hands! Try laying a board down into the thicket to make a walkway deeper into the bushes, allowing you access to the plumpest berries. If you freeze the berries spread out on a cookie sheet, they won't clump together when you put them in a freezer bag for storing. Because Blackberries are so abundant, you don't need to worry about taking too many! (Thank you, Blackberries!)

Brad shows us how to eat Blackberry shoots in the spring.

Raphael chooses only the ripest Blackberries to freeze for later so there will not be any sour surprises.

Try This!

BLACKBERRY SMOOTHIE

Ingredients:
- 1 cup fresh or frozen Blackberries
- 1 cup whole yogourt, milk or non-dairy milk of your choice
- 1 banana, sliced
- 1 teaspoon orange juice concentrate
- 1 cup water

Blend together, and serve right away! Makes four servings to share with your friends.

Nibble This!

The shoots of all the plants in the *Rubus* clan, Blackcaps, Salmonberries, Blackberries and Thimbleberries, are edible and were commonly eaten as spring food in the days before grocery stores. In the spring, when the plants are sending up new growth, you can pluck off these shoots, peel the little stems and eat them raw.

Breah makes some Blackberry smoothie. Katrina Rainoshek

Blackcap Raspberry

Rubus leucodermis

Guild: Thistle, Salal, Red Huckleberry and Fireweed; old clear cuts, disturbed sites

Description

Blackcaps, as they are often called, are not black at all. Their canes, or stems, which have small thorns on them, are a deep, dusty purple-blue. The young berries are red, but they are not ripe and delicious until they are dark purple. Like the Salmonberry, the leaves are alternate, deciduous, toothed and usually in sets of three. The flowers of the Blackcap are small and white and almost unnoticeable.

Blackcap Raspberry.

When the Blackcap berries are ripe, they have a delicious rich flavour like a Marionberry.

Cascara

Rhamnus purshiana

Guild: Alder, Maple, Salmonberry, Sword Fern

Description

Cascara is a small deciduous tree that likes to grow in damp places, at the edges of marshes and in forests. The bark of Cascara, which is smooth, grey and white, looks similar to an Alder or a Maple. The leaves are a good way to tell it apart, as Cascara leaves have smooth **leaf margins**, whereas Alder and Maple leaves have teeth. The branches of Cascara like to swoop up as they grow, and all the twigs end in a little tip of new buds. Cascara flowers in the spring are tiny, yellow and hard to see. In the late summer, they turn into dark-blue berries the size of a marble.

Cascara.

The smooth edges of the Cascara leaf.

Cool Facts about Cascara

The bark of Cascara is so bitter it will make your eyes cross. It is used as a strong medicine that makes you go poop! We call it the Poop Berry Tree. The tiny flowers are a favourite of bees, and when in flower, the whole tree sounds like it is buzzing. The juice of the dark-blue berries makes a great natural face paint and dye.

Rueben wears the paint
of the Cascara berry.

Harvesting Tip
. . . .

Don't, unless you are using them for decoration.

One-Minute Mystery
. . . .

One wintery day I was out for a walk in the woods when I saw what looked like a baby Cascara tree. But it still had its leaves on. Cascara trees are deciduous, so they are supposed to lose their leaves in the fall. As I walked along, I spotted a few more small Cascaras that also had their leaves on. When I looked at the bigger Cascaras in the area, none of them had their leaves on still. What was going on?

ANSWER: These young trees were growing in very shady woods. To gather as much light as possible to turn into food while growing through their first and second winters, some Cascara trees have adapted to keeping their leaves on through the winter. Many deciduous trees have bigger leaves when young than their grown-up relatives, also to gather more light to make into food by photosynthesis. Check out the size of some young Cottonwood leaves!

Guild: Salal, Douglas Fir, Oregon Grape

Description

You may come upon a cluster of Ghost Pipe in some old forest one day and say, "What the heck is this?!" This small fleshy white plant belongs to the Wintergreen clan in the Heath family. When it first pushes up through the rich soil where it likes to grow, it looks almost like some curled-up creature. Then it unfurls and shows its bell-like white-and-black-edged flowers. When Ghost Pipe goes to seed, the flowers turn up to become seed capsules, and the whole plant becomes brown and dried out.

Cool Facts about Ghost Pipe

This is a weird plant. It almost doesn't quite look like a plant, because it is not green. What is it? Ghost Pipe is actually a parasitic plant, meaning it feeds off another living plant instead of making its own food, like most plants do through photosynthesis. In the case of Ghost Pipe, this is done by connecting its small roots to **mycelium** (the underground network of **fungi** roots in the ground), which is then connected to the roots of coniferous trees. This may seem like a roundabout way for this little plant to feed itself, and indeed, it needs a healthy old forest with lots of decaying matter and mycelium to do this. Because of this, you will only find it in mature woods. According to *Plants of Coastal British Columbia*, sometimes this plant is called "Wolf's Pee" in the Straits Salish and Nlaka'pamux languages, because

Ghost Pipe

Monotropa uniflora

Ghost Pipe.

Blue Dog found this Ghost Pipe. He did not find any Wolves, but a few feet away was some fresh Wolf scat.

Harvesting Tip
. . . .

Don't. This plant is rare and sensitive and should only be looked at, not picked.

it grows where a Wolf has peed. Listen for the howl of a Wolf when you see this plant.

Gather 'Round the Ghost Pipe

I find this plant so interesting to look at. Out walking with a friend one day, I spotted a large patch of Ghost Pipe growing beside the trail in a popular park. "Come check this out," I said to my friend. There we were, lying on our bellies looking at the Ghost Pipe, when my daughter's piano teacher happened to walk by with her whole family. "What are you looking at?" they asked. And so I explained all about this strange white plant. Soon enough, they were down on their bellies looking at Ghost Pipe too. Even the grandpa! A few minutes later, the local doctor, who likes to walk his fluffy dog through the park, came along. "What are you looking at?" he asked. Soon he was down on his knees looking at the Ghost Pipe too. There we were—a paramedic, a teacher, a piano teacher and her whole family, and a doctor, all gathered 'round this strange little plant. We never did hear a Wolf howl, but I bet the Ghost Pipe felt pretty special!

"That's weird! Is it even a plant?!"
—Timon, age 8

Guild: Plantain, Dandelion

Common Burdock

Arctium minus

Description

Burdock can grow as tall as me (1.5 metres, or 5 feet) when it is in seed. It has large soft arrow to lance-shaped leaves that grow close to the ground before it sends up its stem in the spring. The flowers of Burdock look almost like Thistles; they are reddish-pink and covered with sharp spikes, lacking any obvious petals. Burdock was introduced from Europe, where it has a long history of being used for medicine. It likes to grow in moist, rich soil in fields, next to gardens and on roadsides.

Burdock.

Cool Facts about Burdock

The flower and seed heads are very sticky and prickly. The plant uses this as a method to spread itself around. Walk through a patch of Burdock, and you will get some seeds stuck to your pants. Dogs and sheep get the seeds tangled in their coats. So with our help, the plant can move around. The little hooks on the end of the "spikes" on the seeds are what inspired the invention of Velcro. Burdock roots are eaten as food in Japan.

Burdock is in the Aster family. Can you figure out why it is related to Dandelion?

Never stick Burdock burrs in someone's hair. They knot even more than chewing gum, and I have had to cut them out of many long beautiful locks!

Try This!
· · · · · · · · · ·

STEALTH BURDOCK TAG

Collect some Burdock seeds. As the day goes along, the challenge is to stick a burr on your friend's or instructor's back without them noticing. Keep your owl eyes on—someone may try to stick one on you!

Sneaky Burdock burrs!

Breah points to the Burdock burrs.

Guild: Red Huckleberry, Blackcap Raspberry, Trailing Blackberry, Bracken Fern

Fireweed

Epilobium angustifolium

Description

Fireweed has alternate lance-shaped leaves all the way up the stem, ending in a spire of bright-magenta flowers at the top. The flowers have four petals. When the petals fall off, Fireweed makes seed pods full of fluffy white seeds. When the pods burst open, this fluff will float over clear-cuts, recently burned areas and clearings.

Cool Facts about Fireweed

Fireweed likes to grow where the environment has been disturbed. It is like nature's bandage, healing the land by using its roots to hold the soil in place when trees and other plants have been taken away. The sea of pink flowers brings beauty to places that otherwise look ravaged from clear-cutting or burning. Fireweed is also edible; the young shoots can be eaten like asparagus. A flavourful tea rich in vitamin C can be made from the leaves, which is good for colds, flus and inflammation. To make tea, harvest the plant before it goes to flower or right at flowering time. Bunch the stems together and hang them to dry. Once they are dry, you can pull off the leaves and flowers and keep them for tea. Fireweed flowers in midsummer, and many beekeepers bring their bees to gather the nectar from the flowers.

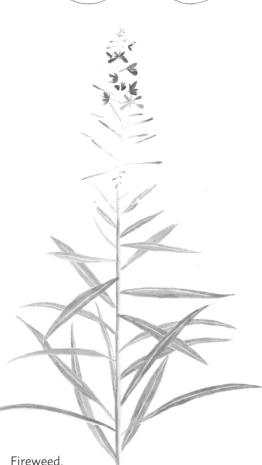

Fireweed.

Field Mint

Mentha arvensis

Guild: Skullcap, Cattail, Willow

Description

Like all plants in the Mint family, Field Mint has a square stem. It likes to grow on stream banks among sedges and grasses with its roots sometimes right in the water. The minty-smelling lance-shaped leaves are opposite, soft and lightly toothed. In the summer, Field Mint has pale-pink flowers that grow like little clusters of trumpets from where the leaves come out of the stem.

"Field Mint makes really yummy tea!"
—Zaylia, age 7

Field Mint.

Try This!

· · · · · · · · ·

SUN TEA

Field Mint makes delicious tea. A super-easy way to make tea in the summer is with the sun! All you need is a large glass jar, a sunny spot, clean water and...mint! Field Mint is best picked just before it flowers in early summer. Use a knife or scissors to cut the mint at the base, then snip or rip the leaves up and put them in your jar. Two to four plants will probably be enough. Put the lid on the jar and place it in a sunny spot for two to three hours. When you come back, just strain out the mint leaves. Chill the tea in the fridge if you want iced tea—perfect on a hot day!

THE MISSING MINT MYSTERY

Be careful where you leave the tea to sit. One day the kids and I had spent the morning gathering Mint and Salmonberries to make a special tea. We decided that the sunny middle of a meadow in the park would be the best place to let it steep while we went off to explore the cool banks of a creek. When we came back, the jar was gone! Vanished like it had never existed! We were so disappointed. "Perhaps a raccoon came and took it," one kid said. "Or a raven swooped down and flew away with it," said another. "I think a UFO came and beamed it up," some-one else offered. We never did find our tea, in my favourite big Mason jar too, but we hope whoever found it enjoyed the delicious wild tea!

Supplies needed:

- Field Mint
- big jar
- water
- scissors or knife to harvest the mint

Gabby and Margret harvesting Field Mint.

Field Mint **97**

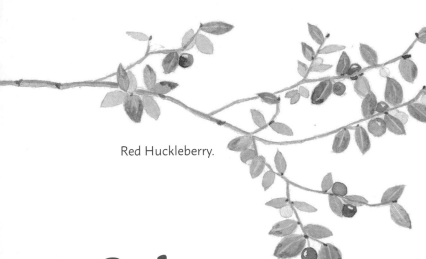

Red Huckleberry.

Red Huckleberry

Vaccinium parvifolium

Oval-Leaved Blueberry

Vaccinium ovalifolium

and Evergreen Huckleberry

Vaccinium ovatum

Guild: Douglas Fir, Sword Fern, Salal; **nurse logs**

Description

There are nine kinds of "blue berries," or plants that belong to the *Vaccinium* clan in the Heath family on the Coast. It is less important to be able to tell them apart than it is to know how to find them, so you can fill your mouth with juicy berries!

The shrubby plants in this family all make edible berries. Mostly, the berries are small, round and blue or black. The Red Huckleberry is…red. The small bell-shaped pinkish-white flowers are happily visited by various bees when they are out in the spring. The alternate leaves of these plants are small and oval, and range from soft and thin in the Red Huckleberry to waxy and slightly toothed in the Evergreen Huckleberry. Most of the *Vacciniums* are deciduous, losing their leaves in the fall, except for the Evergreen Huckleberry, which not only keeps its leaves on all year, but also produces

Evergreen Huckleberry.

If it is a bumper year for Red Huckleberries, you can easily harvest enough berries for a pie. Often little twigs and leaves can fall into your harvesting bucket. An easy way to separate the berries from the other bits is to cover them in water. The leaves and twigs will float to the top and can be poured off, leaving just the clean berries in the bottom of your bucket.

Kids love to eat Huckleberries!

berries late in the summer and keeps them on during the winter. Red Huckleberries like to grow out of old stumps and decaying logs. Blueberries ripen later in the summer and like to grow in the mountains.

One New Year's Day I was on a hike in the snow, and I found a bush loaded with tiny dark-blue Evergreen Huckleberries. A delicious winter treat!

Oval-Leaved Blueberry.

Red Huckleberry   **99**

BERRY FEAST

Huckleberry feast!

Supplies needed:

- bowl or container for harvesting
- yogourt or whipped cream (optional)

On the Coast, late June is a great time for berry eating. With a group of friends, have a berry-harvesting party. Split into two groups, and see which group can harvest the most berries. There are so many berries out this time of year: Red Huckleberries, the last Salmonberries, Trailing Blackberries, Wild Strawberries, Blackcap Raspberries and Thimbleberries. How many varieties can you find? These generous fruits want to be eaten so that their seeds are pooped out and planted elsewhere. Remember to give thanks for the delicious berries. When your bowl or container is full, bring it back and share it with the other group, and they will share with you. This is a great way to show generosity, just like the berry bushes! You may want to eat them with some yogourt or whipped cream or ice cream!

Guild: Douglas Fir, Arbutus, Salal, Sword Fern

Oceanspray

Holodiscus discolor

Description

Oceanspray is common in sunny places or at the edges of the Coastal forest. When this tall deciduous shrub flowers in June, you can see why it is called Oceanspray. The flowers are big white plumes that look like the spray from an ocean wave crashing against the rocks. Because Oceanspray flowers in the middle of summer when many plants are done their flowering, it is an important plant for bees and other pollinators. Sometimes growing as tall as the power lines along the road, Oceanspray puts up long, straight shoots. It has small, many-lobed leaves and smooth grey-brown bark.

Cool Facts about Oceanspray

Oceanspray has also been called Ironwood, because its wood is so hard. It can be used to make many tools, like harpoon shafts and digging sticks. Even today, many people, including my nephew, Raph, make arrows from the long straight shoots of Oceanspray.

Oceanspray.

Oceanspray is in the Rose family. If you look at an Oceanspray flower up close, can you see that the petals are in a multiple of five, like all the flowers in the Rose family?

MAKE YOUR OWN DIGGING STICK

Supplies needed:
- small folding saw

Oceanspray is a generous shrub; it won't mind if you cut a stave (a long straight stick) from its many straight shoots. Digging sticks have been used by Indigenous people on the Coast for thousands of years to help them dig for clams, or for edible roots or bulbs to eat. Choose a stave about as big around as a loonie and as tall as your shoulder. With a small saw, cut it from the plant at the base, or from where it straightens out. You can leave it just like this, or you can make it even stronger by fire-hardening the tip. Once you have a fire going, put your stave about a foot into the fire so that the end heats up. Use your digging stick to help you dig up roots to cook in your fire. (See "Wild Root Roast" on page 151.)

Raph chooses a piece of Oceanspray.

> "I like to choose my Oceanspray arrows carefully. They have to be super straight to fly well. Rose shoots also work for arrows, but be careful of the thorns." —Raph, age 16

Guild: Wild Carrot, Yarrow, Thistle, Bracken Fern, grasses

Oxeye Daisy

Leucanthemum vulgare

Description

Oxeye Daisy, a member of the Aster family, looks like a Daisy should, with white petals around a yellow centre. It is a tall Daisy, up to your knees, with alternate lobed leaves about an inch long coming off the stem up the plant. One plant has many stems and flowers. Before the plant sends up its stalks, it is just a round cluster of leaves growing close to the ground. Oxeye Daisy likes to grow in fields, on roadsides and in open cleared areas.

Nibble This!

The leaves of Oxeye Daisy are edible, and the young leaves are especially sweet, tasting a bit like vanilla. You can eat them as a snack or add them to a salad.

Cool Facts about Oxeye Daisy

Oxeye Daisy is native to Europe but now widely spread across North America. Birds like Finches like to eat the seeds in the late summer.

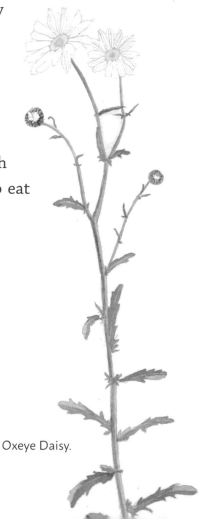

Oxeye Daisy.

"Oxeye Daisies look like fried eggs on a stem."
—Breah, age 10

THE LONGEST DAISY CHAIN EVER!

Use Oxeye Daisies to make a daisy chain. Use your fingernail or the tip of a sharp knife to make a slit two inches from the end of the stem, then slide in another daisy and make a slit in the end of that stem and so on. Work as a team to make the longest chain ever!

Rueben, Maya and Breah made a 25-foot-long daisy chain!

Guild: Self-Heal, Buttercup, Dandelion

Description

There are two kinds of Plantain common to the Coast. English Plantain (*Plantago lanceolata*) has long lance-shaped leaves. Common Plantain (*Plantago major*) has round to oblong leaves. Both of these plants have deeply parallel-veined leaves, which give them their other name, Ribwort. They are low-growing plants that often don't die back in the Coastal winter. In the summer, they send up many stems with their very un-flower-like flowers. These flowers form small green, then brown, heads on the stems, and then send out what looks like a little white halo around each flower head. Plantain likes to grow in moist rich soil in gardens, meadows, cracks in the sidewalk and open clearings.

Oval Leaf Plantain.

Cool Facts about Plantain

Plantain is a gently soothing healing plant with **styptic** properties similar to Yarrow, which means it stops bleeding. The kids in my nature school know to go look for Plantain right away if someone gets a bee or nettle sting. "Found some!" Zaylia calls, as she comes running over with three leaves to give to Gabby for her sting.

Plantain (Ribwort)

English Plantain or Narrowleaf
Plantago lanceolata

Common or Oval Leaf Plantain
Plantago major

English Plantain.

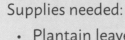

MAKE YOUR OWN HEALING PLANTAIN SALVE

Supplies needed:

- Plantain leaves
- olive, avocado, apricot kernel or other kind of whole oil
- old newspaper
- some small jars
- lavender essential oil (optional)
- small saucepan you don't mind getting oily
- beeswax
- measuring cup
- kitchen scale

Plantain salve is good to have on hand for those times when you can't just go pick some. It is healing both to bug bites and Nettle stings, but also to dry and chapped skin, rashes, diaper rash, eczema and slow-healing cuts. Making the salve is a two-step process.

First you will need to make an oil from the Plantain by harvesting some leaves when they are fresh. Then make an oil from them by following the directions for Cottonwood (page 36). Alternatively, you can dry the leaves you pick and make an oil in your blender by adding seven parts of oil to one part of dried Plantain leaves. Blend the leaves in the oil for about fifteen minutes. The blender will heat the oil up and extract the medicine

Breah harvesting Plantain leaf to make oil with. Katrina Rainoshek

Measuring the Plantain oil for making salve. Katrina Rainoshek

from the Plantain. Be careful—the blender might be hot. Strain the plant bits from the oil.

Now you are ready to make the salve:

- Lay down old newspaper on the counter to make cleaning up easier.
- Have your small jars clean and dry, ready to use.
- You can add a drop or two of lavender essential oil to the bottom of each jar if you like. This is also good for burns, bites and wound healing, and it smells good and keeps the salve from spoiling.
- Put your strained oil in a small pot on low heat on the stove. You will need 125 millilitres (½ cup) of oil to make about 150 millilitres (5 ounces) of salve.
- Cut your beeswax into small bits so it melts faster. You need 28 grams (1 ounce) of beeswax for every 250 millilitres (1 cup) of oil you use.
- Let the wax dissolve into the oil on the stove, stirring once in a while and making sure it does not boil.

Plantain has been called "White Man's Footstep" because it was noticed that the plant grew wherever the first European settlers passed through.

Plantain (Ribwort)   **107**

Naomi and Chantel pour
Plantain salve. Katrina Rainoshek

Our finished plantain salve!
Katrina Rainoshek

- When the wax is completely melted into the oil, you can carefully pour this into your jars. You can also pour it into a measuring cup with a spout to make pouring it into your small jars easier.
- Let the jars of salve cool where they are without moving them.
- When they are completely cool, put their lids on and make some decorative labels, maybe with a drawing of the plants you used.
- Your equipment will need to be washed with very hot water and lots of soap to get the oil and wax off!
- Carry your Plantain salve in your hiking bag or first aid kit, use it at home, or give it away for gifts.

Guild: Douglas Fir, Cedar, Sword Fern, Huckleberry

Salal

Description

You can't really walk anywhere in a Coastal forest without meeting Salal. Growing up to your knees or even up to your neck, with thick glossy leaves, Salal forms a thick **understory** in most wet Douglas Fir forests. In the spring, Salal makes small bell-shaped white flowers, similar to its Heath family cousins, Arbutus, Huckleberry and Blueberry. When August arrives, these flowers have turned into dark-purple berries. If we have had a damp summer, the berries are plump, sweet and easy to collect. If it has been a very dry summer, the berries are small and mealy.

Gaultheria shallon

Cool Facts about Salal

Salal has been an important food plant on the Coast for thousands of years. Families still pick large baskets full of them and then mash them and dry them in cakes to eat in the winter. In the time before money, these cakes were both given away as gifts and traded for food or items that people needed.

Salal.

Bumblebees are one of the main pollinators of Salal. On a warm day in spring, when the plants flower, you can sit quietly and hear the low hum of the bumblebees as they fly from flower to flower gathering nectar.

Ayanna enjoying a Salal snack.

Katrina Rainoshek

The Plants Are Lonely

I was once on a walk with W̱SÁNEĆ Elder John Elliott in a beautiful inlet near Victoria. He showed me why his people called the area their "refrigerator" in the old days, because there was so much food. When the tide was low, you could go gather clams, and there were deer to hunt, fish to catch and many berries to pick. "But now," he said, "the plants and berries are lonely. Not enough people are out picking them. The plants like being spoken to, especially in our language. That is the language they know. They like the sound of kids laughing and of people singing. Even the Salal doesn't make berries like it used to."

Salal berries.

Nibble This!

. . . .

Salal is fun to eat on walks and hikes, because the whole little branch the berries grow on comes off at once, and you can nibble off the berries as you go. Pick a whole bunch to share with your family or friends when you find a good patch. When you toss away the branches after, you are not littering, because they came from the forest!

Try This!

MAKE YOUR OWN BERRY CAKES

Supplies needed:

- Salal berries
- bucket or container
- big bowl
- potato masher or big wooden spoon
- cookie sheets or dehydrator

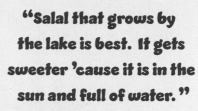

"Salal that grows by the lake is best. It gets sweeter 'cause it is in the sun and full of water."
—Felix, age 11

Because Salal berries are not very juicy, they dry more easily than other berries. Find a good patch of plump Salal berries and fill your picking bucket. When you have a few buckets' worth, take the berries to the kitchen and put them in a big bowl. With a potato masher or big wooden spoon, mash and mush the berries until they are a pulp. Once they are mashed, spread them out or make cookie-sized circles on the screen of a food dehydrator and dry on the fruit setting, or on a screen in the sun. Once they are totally dry, store in an airtight container.

Naomi harvests Salal to make berry cakes. Katrina Rainoshek

They will keep for a long time and make great snacks when packed for hikes or lunches. They are full of good things for your body and are yummy too! Beware, though—when you smile, you may have blue teeth.

Sundew

Drosera rotundifolia

Sundew.

Guild: Sphagnum Moss, Northern Water Horehound, Hardhack, Cattail; nurse logs

Description

Sundew is an insect-eating plant that grows where it is wet, on lake and marsh edges and in Sphagnum Moss bogs. I often see it growing on trees that have fallen into lakes and become like little islands with plants growing from them. Sundew is a small plant, easy to overlook at first, just as tall as your longest finger. It grows in clusters on logs and moss. The leaves are on the end of the stems and are flat and round with sticky tentacles covered in clear goo protruding from the leaves. This is where flies get trapped and eaten. In the summer, Sundew makes little white flowers that open only in bright sun.

Cool Facts about Sundew

Sundew is related to the Venus Flytrap (*Dionaea muscipula*), and what is cooler than a **carnivorous**, insect-eating plant?! Sundews eat flies and other insects to add to their diet, because they have a hard time photosynthesizing, or

Harvesting Tip
. . . .

These plants are rare to uncommon and grow in sensitive ecosystems. Don't pick them.

"If I could turn myself into any plant, I would be a Sundew and eat dragons! Or dragonflies, at least."
—Rueben, age 9

making food from the sun. They do this by trapping insects in their sticky pads; then a chemical in the goo causes the insect to break down and be absorbed by the plant. These tiny and uncommon plants have many uses, including as a love charm in Haida culture, as a wart remover, for curdling milk to make cheese, and in cough medicine. Eating Sundew supposedly turns your pee a different colour.

I wouldn't want to be this Damselfly being devoured by the Sundew!

One of the best ways to get up close to Sundew to watch them eat flies without disturbing their habitats is to canoe or swim to where they grow on logs fallen into a lake or marsh. I took this picture when I took off my shoes and socks and balanced on a fallen Cedar log.

Although Sundew has no teeth, I have even seen it eat dragonflies!

Sundew   **113**

Thimbleberry

Rubus parviflorus

> "The flavour of Thimbleberries is so rich, complex and hard to describe...like a rare delicacy."
>
> —Naomi, age 11

Guild: Bracken Fern, Bitter Cherry, Red Huckleberry, Snowberry, Oceanspray

Description

Thimbleberry...*mmmmmm*, yum. To find these most delicious berries, look for plants with large, soft, alternate **palmate** (maple-shaped) leaves. Thimbleberries grow about as tall as a six-year-old in open, dry clearings. In the spring, they make white flowers with a yellow centre about the size of a toonie. In July, the flowers turn into domed-shaped bright-red berries about the size of a small Raspberry. Even though these berries are small, their flavour is big. Thimbleberry is cousin to Blackberry, in the Rose family and the *Rubus* clan.

Thimbleberry.

Harvesting Tip

. . . .

The berries are soft and don't do well being carried around, so it's best to use your mouth and tummy when gathering them. That said, the large soft leaves can be folded to make a little basket to carry the berries in. If you do want to keep some for later, you can make a mush of them, on their own or mixed with whatever other berries are ripe, and spread it out on the sheets of a dehydrator to make berry fruit leather.

Stella and Westy know the best way to eat Thimbleberries—right off their fingers like thimbles!

Thimbleberry   115

Wild Strawberry

Fragaria virginiana

Woodland Strawberry
Fragaria vesca

Coastal Strawberry
Fragaria chiloensis

Wild Strawberry.

Guild: Self-Heal, Trailing Blackberry, Bracken Fern; grassy clearings, meadows, roadsides

Description
Wild Strawberries look much like their bigger garden-variety cousins. They have soft green leaves in sets of three, white flowers with yellow centres and, in early summer, small heart-shaped red fruits. Strawberries spread by sending out **runners**, long stems that creep across the ground, finding new spots to grow. Like so many yummy fruits, Strawberries are in the Rose family.

Cool Facts about Wild Strawberry
There are two other kinds of Strawberries that grow on the Coast as well. One is called Woodland Strawberry (*Fragaria vesca*), and the other Coastal Strawberry (*Fragaria chiloensis*). Coastal Strawberry is one of the hardiest little plants I have ever seen. I once saw it growing at the northernmost tip of Vancouver Island, where the storm waves can get higher than a two-storey house and smash against the rocks with so much force it seems the waves would break your bones. But there on the rocks, covered in the spray from these giant waves, were the little Coastal Strawberries. They have thicker, more leathery leaves than their cousins, and the

berries have a salty-sweet flavour. They would win any contest of strength against their woodland or wild cousins.

Strawberry Wolves

It was a windy day on a little island off the west coast of Vancouver Island when I found the most amazing patch of Wild Strawberries. They were growing next to a little creek that seeped out from the thick Spruce forest. After I'd been hiking for days with only raisins for fruit, the fresh sweetness of the Strawberries was amazing.

I was so lost in hunting for berries that I was surprised all of a sudden by the sound of footsteps. Not the sound of a human's heavy two-footed trudge. It was the sound of four light feet. I turned, and there was a Wolf running right toward me! Surprised by the Wolf's sudden appearance, I blurted out, "Hey Wolf! Stop!" And it did. As quickly as it had been running toward me, it turned right around and went back the way it had come.

The Wolf was about as tall as my thigh and had scraggly light-grey-and-blond fur. My heart beat quickly, for although I knew Wolves very rarely hurt humans, it was still startling to have a wild animal run right toward me. The wind had been blowing my scent away from it and I had been crouched down, so the Wolf had neither smelled nor seen me. As I looked around, wondering if the Wolf would come back, I noticed something I would have seen earlier had my attention not just been on the Strawberries. There, about 3 metres (15 feet) away from me, was the

Nibble This!

Although they are small, Wild Strawberries are packed with flavour! The best way to eat them is by lying on your belly or crawling around on your hands and knees, so you can find the little red fruits hiding under their leaves.

"Wild Strawberries are one of my favourite plants because they are juicy and sweet."
—Harriet, age 10

The delicate harvest of Wild Strawberries, just before the wolves came.

mostly eaten skeleton of an animal. Gosh! I was right in the Wolf's kitchen. Feeling kind of bad about interrupting the Wolf's dinner time, I reluctantly headed up the beach to find a campsite.

No sooner had I gone just a few paces away than I heard the sound of footsteps again on the pebbles. Sure enough, another Wolf was heading full tilt straight at me! Startled, again I yelled out, "Stop, Wolf!" Equally surprised to see me, this Wolf, who had black fur, also turned around and disappeared into the forest.

With a racing heart, I did my best to set up my camp for the night. Every time the waves rolled the pebbles on the beach, I was sure it was another Wolf. Just as the dawn chorus of birdsong started up, I was awoken by the sound of footsteps going past my tent. I lay still and quiet, hoping I wasn't in the Wolves' way. Were they going to gnaw on that rib cage?

When I finally crawled out of my tent, I went to see if the Wolves had moved the carcass. They hadn't, and there was no sign that the Wolves had touched it in the night. So I went to find some Strawberries for breakfast, and what did I see? There were Wolf prints all around the Strawberry patch! So this is what the Wolves had wanted all along. The sweet goodness of ripe Wild Strawberries!

Guild: Hardhack, Crab Apple, Salmonberry, Cattails; stream sides, shores, wet clearings, marshes

Hooker's Willow.

Description

Hooker's, Scouler's and Pacific Willow are the three most common Willows in our area, but there are actually over ten different species of Willow on the Coast. These Willows grow into small deciduous trees with supple, bendy branches and alternate leaves. Many of the Willows make bright splashes of colour in the winter landscape with their golden and red bark. Here are some ways to tell them apart:

	Hooker's Willow	Scouler's Willow	Pacific Willow
HABITAT	Often grows by beaches or marsh edges	Grows in thickets in wetlands	Grows by rivers or standing in water
HABITS	Pussy willows before leaves	Catkins are silky and stand up	Catkins with leaves
LEAVES	Small oval leaves with soft bottoms	More oblong than Hooker's	Long, pointed and smooth
HEIGHT	Up to 6 m tall	Up to 12 m tall	Up to 12 m tall

Willow

Hooker's Willow
Salix hookeriana

Scouler's Willow
Salix scouleriana

Pacific Willow
Salix lucida

The Latin word for Willow, *Salix*, means to grow by the water. This is why I named my outdoor school Salix School, because kids are growing up near the water and are learning to be flexible.

Cool Facts about Willow

Willows are found all over the northern hemisphere, and their bendy branches have been used for centuries as a material for making baskets. Willow doesn't mind having some of its branches cut down; it just sprouts new ones. Basket makers do this by **coppicing** (cutting near the base of the tree) when they harvest branches, to keep young, straight branches forming every year. Willow medicine has a long use around the world for headaches and pain and is now made into the common drug called aspirin.

Pacific Willow.

Try This!

. . . .

WILLOW CROWNS

Supplies needed:

- Willow trees
- hand pruners
- ribbon or string (optional)

Get to know the bendy quality of Willow by cutting a straight shoot as tall as yourself. This can be worked into a circular shape, weaving the ends together to form a crown. Collect other flowers, plants or feathers to weave into the crown. This might be a good thing to wear when using your magic wand and saying the magic words of Latin names.

"I like Willows, because you can often find birds' nests in them."
—Sophia, age 11

Look at the Willow crowns we made! Katrina Rainoshek

Yarrow

Achillea millefolium

Yarrow.

Guild: Sticky Gumweed, Tansy, Wild Carrot; meadows, fields, beach sides

Description

Yarrow is a perennial plant that grows to about two feet tall. It starts out as a bunch of feathery, Fern-like leaves that are soft and smell sweet. In the late spring it sends up its woody stem, and in the summer it grows a crown of small white flowers. It might be hard to tell, but if you look up close, you can see that Yarrow is in the Aster family, even though its white umbels of flowers make it look like it is in the Carrot family.

Cool Facts about Yarrow

Yarrow is said to be the most widely recognized medicinal plant in the world. Not only that, it is one of the oldest plants known to be used as medicine. Yarrow has many uses as a medicine, but perhaps the one most useful to you will be for cuts. The Latin name for Yarrow, *Achillea*, is named for the Greek hero Achilles, who was said to have healed his warriors with Yarrow.

In Spain, archaeologists found a 50,000-year-old Neanderthal skull with Yarrow still stuck in its teeth! Must have been a bad toothache.

YARROW FIRST AID

Yarrow is what is called a styptic, meaning it stops bleeding. When I teach knife skills to kids, I also teach them how to find Yarrow. If they cut themselves while carving, they know how to stop the bleeding.

Here is what you do:

"Ouch!" someone yells, when their knife slips. Tell them to stay sitting down, hold on to the cut finger with their other

Chantel harvests Yarrow for first aid. Katrina Rainoshek

Yarrow   **123**

Margret uses Yarrow for first aid.

RED stands for **R**est, **E**levate, **D**irect pressure.

hand, apply pressure and then raise it. This is called **RED**, which stands for **R**est (stay sitting down), **E**levate (raise the injured part above the heart to slow the blood flow) and apply **D**irect pressure, which also slows the bleeding. Then ask someone who knows what Yarrow (or Plantain, which is also a styptic) looks like to gather a few leaves from a clean place nearby. Get the person with the cut to lightly chew up the leaves (but not swallow them) and then quickly let go of the cut and place the chewed-up leaves over the site. Reapply pressure, holding the leaves in place. After five minutes, have a look, and the bleeding will most likely have stopped. Then wash the cut with clean water and apply a bandage.

Note: This method is safe first aid for small superficial cuts, not deep gashes or anything that is bleeding a lot. If the bleeding hasn't slowed or stopped after five minutes, the cut may need stitches, and the hurt person should be taken to a clinic or the emergency department.

Summer Scavenger Hunt
. . . .

1. Collect three plants that can be used as medicine. Is there one that is good for cuts?
2. Find four examples of deciduous trees.
3. Collect three round stones: a white one, a black one and a green one.
4. Can you find any berries in the *Rubus* clan?
5. Find four plants that armour themselves with spikes, thorns, prickles or stingers.
6. Find two plants in the *Vaccinium* clan. Are they making berries?
7. Collect three flowers. Look at them closely. How many petals do they have? Can you guess what family they are in?
8. Sit in a patch of shade. Which direction is the shade pointing?
9. Find three examples of a plant that has "gone to seed."
10. Collect three different types of grasses.

Summer flower scavenger hunt.

Autumn

Autumn usually begins golden and ends grey. Leaves of deciduous trees turn yellow, orange and red, then brown, and fall to the earth. Seeds are ripe and released to the ground, where they wait through winter to sprout in the spring. Late fruit is ripe and sweetens in the cold. The energy of the plants is down in their roots. This is a good time to harvest roots for food and medicine.

Whose feet are these?

Arbutus (Madrone)

Arbutus menziesii

Guild: Douglas Fir, Bigleaf Maple, Yerba Buena, Oregon Grape

> When my nephew was little, he called Arbutus trees "ar-beauty-ous," because they are so beautiful!

Description

With a smooth twisted trunk and peeling papery skin of gold, green, red and brown, this is a wonderful tree to touch and look at. Arbutus can grow up to 30 metres (100 feet), which is about as high as a ten-storey building. The leaves are oblong, thick, waxy and green. In late spring, clusters of small bell-shaped white flowers, like those of its cousins in the Heath family, cover the branches and smell sweet. Sometimes you can hear a buzzing sound coming from the trees, as many bees gather the flowers' nectar. The flowers turn into bright-red-orange berries in the fall and winter. Arbutus trees are often crooked, twisted and growing at funny angles. They like to grow out over the sea from dry banks or in clusters on high, dry ridges.

Cool Facts about Arbutus

In this **bioregion**, Arbutus is the only **broad-leaved** native evergreen tree. This means that when all the deciduous trees have dropped their leaves, the Arbutus leaves are still green. Instead of losing their leaves all at once, they keep growing new leaves while losing old leaves throughout the year.

Arbutus flower.

Autumn   127

MAKE A GARLAND OR NECKLACE

Supplies needed:
- Arbutus berries
- needle and thread

Arbutus berries are fun to gather in late autumn or winter and string with a needle and thread for Christmas tree garlands or a necklace. When you are done with them, you can remove the berries from the string and leave them outside for the birds to eat.

Tosh makes an Arbutus berry necklace.

The bunches of berries sometimes blow down to the ground after a windstorm. This makes these high-growing berries easier to harvest. If you are harvesting them right off the tree, make sure you leave enough for the birds!

The berries are an important source of food for birds in the winter, and you can often see Robins darting about, gulping down the fruits when there is not much else to eat. People can also eat the berries, but they are dry, mealy and not very sweet.

Arbutus or Madrone berry.

Guild: Garry Oak, Shooting Star, Chocolate Lily, Sea Blush, Death Camas, Buttercup

Description

When Camas is in flower in April and May, it is hard to miss. But other times of the year, only a careful eye can see it. In the early spring, the leaves of Camas come up, looking like thick leaves of grass and very similar to Bluebells and Daffodils, which are taking over some Camas meadows. When Camas blooms, the beautiful purple-blue (and, rarely, white) six-petalled flowers shimmer in moist meadows where it likes to grow. Lie down on your tummy to see the golden-yellow pollen the bees love to gather. After the petals fall from the flower, green seed pods are left, which then turn brown and papery as the summer sun dries them out.

Great Camas is usually taller, with fewer but larger flowers, and blooms slightly later than Common Camas. Great Camas wraps its petals around the seed pods as they form, to give the seeds extra warmth. This helps them ripen in time before the seeds fall in the autumn rains.

Cool Facts about Camas

Camas was once so abundant in the meadows of Vancouver Island that, from a distance, the flowers

Camas

Common Camas
Camassia quamash

Great Camas
Camassia leichtlinii

Use **CAUTION** because of look-alike Death Camas.

Great Camas.

"Camas is one of my favourite flowers, because the colour of blue is so deep."

—Breah, age 10

There was a beautiful Camas meadow that I used to visit as a kid just outside the city of Victoria. When I drive by now and see the Home Depot and Costco built on top of the meadow, I want to cry. Do you think the bulbs will wait underground for hundreds of years to sprout again once those buildings are gone? I hope so!

shone like a lake. These meadows were tended carefully by the Coastal Indigenous people, who depended on them for hunting deer and gathering Camas bulbs for food. The meadows were maintained by setting a quick fire to them in late summer and by weeding out plants like Death Camas and removing rocks. Camas was an important food. It tastes much like potatoes, and, in harvest time, whole families set up camp by the meadows to harvest sacks full of the bulbs. The bulbs were dug with digging sticks and only the biggest ones taken, leaving the smallest ones to be replanted to grow for the next year, thus keeping the Camas always growing. Camas was usually harvested just after it flowered so that it wouldn't be confused with the very poisonous Death Camas, whose bulbs look very similar to Camas bulbs.

Despite being beautiful and an important food, Camas is now a rare plant. When settlers came from Europe, they wanted to graze their cows in the lush Camas meadows, which destroyed many meadows. After that, the meadows were turned into farms and then paved over to make room for roads, parking lots, houses and stores.

The best places to see Camas and other wild Lilies these days are Beacon Hill and Uplands Park in Victoria. Many local people are working to protect what is left of the Garry Oak ecosystems where these Lilies grow. And once again, the Songhees and W̱SÁNEĆ people of southern Vancouver Island are tending Camas meadows and harvesting the bulbs to cook and share with their communities.

SPREAD THE SEEDS

As you walk through a Camas meadow in late summer, the dry seed pods rattle with their ripe seeds. Break open one of these papery-brown seed pods to see the little shiny round black seeds inside. These seeds can be collected and planted, helping to spread these beautiful rare flowers. Shake the seeds from the pods into a little plastic bag or envelope. Make sure you write on it what the seeds are! You can either plant the seeds in a planting flat in garden soil, plant them directly in your garden or take them and sprinkle them in places where the Lilies like to grow, like mossy outcroppings and meadows. This is best done in the fall, so the seeds have the important cold of winter to get ready for spring. The first few years of growth look like small blades of grass, and it can take up to seven years before these Lilies flower, so mark where you plant them well and be patient! Fawn Lily and Chocolate Lily seeds can be collected and spread the same way.

The beauty of a Camas meadow in full bloom.

Blue Elderberry.

Elder

Red Elder

Sambucus racemosa ssp. *pubens*

Blue Elder

Sambucus caerulea

Guild: Douglas Fir, Bigleaf Maple, Red Huckleberry, Sword Fern

Description

These deciduous shrubs like to grow in moist forest clearings and along roadsides. Their long, pointy leaves grow opposite

Red Elder flower.

each other on the branch. The shoots of Elder grow straight up. When Elder gets really old, its trunk and branches get gnarled and twisted. Red Elder flowers in May and sets its fruit in midsummer, whereas Blue Elder flowers in June, and its berries are ripe in September. The flowers are small white clusters that look like umbrellas. The berries form clumps of tiny round fruits of red or dark blue.

Cool Facts about Elder

All types of Elder were, and still are, an important food for people on the Coast. Red Elderberries are always cooked; otherwise, they are poisonous. Many birds love to eat the berries as well, and you can often see flocks of Cedar Waxwings in these shrubs when the berries are ripe. The stems of Elder are filled with squishy pith and can easily be hollowed out. You can make beads by cutting the Elder stem crosswise into little rounds with a small saw. You can also cut a section as long as your hand to hollow out from one end as a straw or a place to put secret notes.

Try This!
. . . .

MAKE YOUR OWN ELDERBERRY SYRUP

Supplies needed:
- Blue Elderberries
- picking bucket
- ladder (maybe)
- honey
- pot
- strainer or sieve

Black and Blue Elderberries have long been used as medicine. These berries are very high in vitamin C and are really good for colds and flus. But the best part is that the syrup is so yummy, you can pour it on your pancakes! Collect the Blue Elderberries in the fall when they are ripe. They often grow up high on the branches, so you will need a ladder, or a long rake to hook the

When I harvest Elderberries, I often stand on the roof of my truck to pick them. Breah thinks this is fun, but kind of embarrassing. It must be worth it, because once in a while she pretends to feel a bit sick, just for a sip of Elderberry syrup.

Adobe Stock, Norkaph

Elder   **133**

branches down. Remember to leave some berries for the birds. A 500-millilitre bucket will make enough syrup for the year. Rinse the berries when you get home, then put them in a heavy-bottomed saucepan. Cover them with twice as much honey and turn the pot on low on the stove. Let this simmer all day, without letting it boil. When it is done, strain off the pulp from the berries, and put the honey in a jar. This is your Elderberry syrup! You shouldn't need to keep it in the fridge, but keep it somewhere cool and dark. The leftover berries that you strained off are delicious when made into tea—just pour boiling water over them, let them sit for ten minutes and drink!

Picking the berries off to make Elderberry syrup.

Guild: Arbutus, Douglas Fir, Scotch Broom, Camas, Fawn Lily, Snowberry

An Oak tree in flower.

Description

Garry Oak is a deciduous tree, the only Oak native to our region. This tree takes on two different forms, depending on where it is growing. In rich soil and on valley bottoms, the trees grow straight trunks up to 1.5 metres (5 feet) wide with huge **canopies** of twisted limbs. They can grow up to 23 metres (75 feet) tall in an open sunny spot. If the Oaks are growing on a hillside with rocky soil, as they often do, they grow slowly, with twisting, gnarly trunks and limbs. Sometimes these trees even grow right along the ground in places where the wind sculpts them to the rock. Like many deciduous trees, the bark of the Garry Oak gets thick and furrowed with age. The alternate leaves are deeply lobed and waxy. They are the last of the deciduous leaves to come out in the spring and the last leaves to fall from the trees in the autumn. Autumn is when you will see the acorns drop to the ground. Garry Oak

Garry Oak
(Oregon White Oak)

Quercus garryana

This used to be a Garry Oak forest!

Garry Oak.

"I love Oak trees, because they are so gnarly, but somehow also so handsome. They grow so big! I wish there were more of them." —Breah, age 10

likes to grow with lots of light and will die if it gets shaded out by other trees. This happens often, as Douglas Fir likes to grow in the same areas, but it grows much faster.

Cool Facts about Garry Oak

The Garry Oak grows in only a few places in our Coastal home. The Comox Valley on Vancouver Island is the northernmost part of its range, while to the south it grows all the way into Northern California. Garry Oak is part of a rare and beautiful ecosystem that supports many rare wildflowers, like Camas, and endangered animals, like the Western Bluebird. Before European settlers came to the Coast, these ecosystems were maintained by the Coastal Indigenous people with a sophisticated technique of setting fire to the area. These were controlled fires, which would be fast and hot enough to burn out only the young Fir trees and other shrubs. This burning kept the land open for the growth of wildflowers and Oak trees and for easy hunting. Now that this practice is banned, Garry Oak meadows are shaded out by faster-growing trees like Douglas Fir and thick stands of Scotch Broom. Because Garry Oak grows where people want to live and drive, many Oak meadows have been paved over to become parking lots for big-box stores, housing tracts and roads. If you would like to see these beautiful and rare ecosystems, there are still a few parks around the city of Victoria that show what the original Garry Oak meadows looked like.

GROW YOUR OWN OAKS

Supplies needed:

- acorns
- bucket full of water
- planting pots
- potting soil
- label for plant pots

Tending the baby Oak

trees. Katrina Rainoshek

Oak trees want to grow here, and they can do so easily with your help. Find a big, old Oak tree with lots of acorns. You can collect these off the ground when they drop, from mid-September until late November. Sometimes the acorns are rotten or have been eaten on the inside by little bugs. A way to tell which acorns are still good is to drop them all in a pail of water. The ones that are good will sink to the bottom of the bucket, and the ones that are not good will float to the top. The good ones can be planted directly outside—bury them in about six inches of soil in a sunny spot. Or you can plant them in pots, which makes them easy to be given away as gifts or carried elsewhere to plant out. Oaks grow a long **taproot**, so it is best to plant them out within their first year to avoid disturbing the root. They are a slow-growing tree, but with some regular watering and a lot of patience, you will be rewarded with knowing you have helped another Oak grow in a world where they are so rare.

Oak trees are great trees to plant these days with our uncertain climate. They grow well through long dry spells but don't mind if it rains all summer either.

Garry Oak   **137**

Licorice Fern

Polypodium glycyrrhiza

Licorice fern.

Guild: Bigleaf Maple, Snowberry; decaying logs, rocky outcrops

Description

Licorice Fern is a sweet little Fern whose leaves rarely get bigger than six inches. Its fronds taper into a long triangle, and the ends of the leaves appear to be rounded. The **sori**, or spore pods, on the back side of the leaves are a rusty-brown colour. Licorice Fern likes to grow on old mossy Bigleaf Maples, giving the trees a hanging garden look. It will also grow on mossy bluffs, on decaying logs and in rich soil.

Sophia cuts up Licorice Fern roots. Katrina Rainoshek

Licorice fern roots for tea. Katrina Rainoshek

Cool Facts about Licorice Fern

Licorice Fern is called Licorice Fern because it tastes like... licorice! The root is used as a medicinal tea for sore throats and colds.

Licorice Fern likes to grow on mossy bluffs and outcroppings, which are moist in the spring and fall but dry out completely in the summer. When this happens, it looks as if the Fern is totally dead, all brown and dry. But when the autumn rains come back, the Fern pops right back to life, becoming green and lush again.

Nibble This!

Because Licorice Ferns grow in sensitive ecosystems where moss can take many years to grow, it is important to treat the Ferns and their habitat carefully. If you would like to try some root to nibble on or make a soothing tea, choose a spot where the Fern grows abundantly and you can get at it without wrecking the moss around it. Using your hands, gently feel for the root, which is just below the surface. Use a small knife to cut out a section of the root as long as your finger, in between two stems. Carefully cover up the spot again so it looks like you were never there. You can nibble on the root fresh or make a tea; just cut the root up into small pieces and boil it for ten minutes.

Mullein

Verbascum thapsus

> **"You don't want to confuse Mullein with Foxglove or Comfrey when you use it for toilet paper! Trust me, I know."**
> —Philippa, age 40

Guild: Foxglove, Yarrow; dry disturbed sites

Description

Mullein likes to grow in disturbed soils. Look for the great, tall spires of yellow flowers on roadsides, on cleared land, in empty lots and in dry, **arid** places. Mullein is a **biannual**, meaning it lives for two years. The first year it is a basal growth of soft-grey-green leaves, which sometimes grow bigger than your arm. In its second year, a flower stalk emerges, growing straight up, covered in soft, fuzzy leaves and ending in a spire of small yellow flowers. Some Mullein can grow up to 3 metres (9 feet) tall with multiple flower stalks that branch off, so that they look like the great Saguaro Cactus (*Carnegiea gigantea*) of the desert!

The leaves of the first year's growth can look similar to the leaves of Foxglove, which is in the same family but is poisonous, so be sure to look closely before handling. Foxglove leaves are not as soft or thick as Mullein, nor do they have the same thick veins in the leaves. The leaves of Mullein grow in a basal form, whereas Foxglove leaves grow alternate.

Mullein.

Making Mullein torches.

Katrina Rainoshek

Cool Facts about Mullein

Mullein was brought to North America by early settlers from Europe. It has long been used as a medicine in both places. Like the softness of the leaves, it gives softness to a sore throat or cough when drunk as a tea. Mullein has also been called Torch Plant, because the flower stalks were used as lanterns before people had electricity or even candles! The thick, soft leaves are great to stop blisters in your shoes and make a very nice "hiker's toilet paper."

This is a great plant to grow because it doesn't need any watering throughout the dry summers, and it looks majestic in a garden.

Harvesting Tip

Where Mullein grows, it is usually abundant enough to harvest with ease. If you are using the leaves for soft shoe insoles or for hiker's toilet paper, just break the leaves off at the base. Mullein grows easily from seed, so if you want your very own Mullein patch, just collect some of their tiny black seeds at the end of summer and sprinkle them where you want them to grow. The seeds will sprout the next spring and grow into big plants the year after whose flowers the bees will love!

Crab Apple.

Pacific Crab Apple

Malus fusca

Guild: Hawthorn, Cascara, Spirea, Rose, Willow, Salal

Description

Crab Apple is a small deciduous tree, growing not more than 10 metres (30 feet) high. In the winter, when it has no leaves, the tree looks almost spooky, because the branches grow so twisted and irregular. Once May comes along, the Crab Apple is covered in tiny clusters of white blossoms that attract many pollinators. By fall, the flowers have turned into bunches of small fruit.

When the fruit is green, it is very sour, but if you wait until late fall, after the first frost, the fruit turns brown, gets a little mushy and is very tasty.

Crab Apple is easily confused with Hawthorn, which also has twisty irregular branches, small fruits, scaly bark when old and scalloped leaves. Crab Apple can have a wide variety of leaf shapes, which can make it hard to identify only by the leaves. The fruits on Crab Apple are bigger than those of Hawthorn and are green, yellow or brown. Crab Apple likes to grow where it can have "wet feet," at the edge of marshes, lakes or shores, or where there is a little underground water.

Cool Facts about Crab Apple

Crab Apples were such an important food for Indigenous people on the Coast that specific trees and stands of trees were reserved for the families of chiefs. Once the chief's family had harvested enough Crab Apples to store for the winter, then other families would be allowed to harvest from those trees. To make the trees easier to harvest, it was a common practice for people to break the tops of the tree over, so that it would keep growing but be easier to reach. Some of these trees can still be spotted in old harvesting sites around marshes. If you see a Crab Apple with a bent-over top, it is possible someone was there harvesting the fruit many years ago. Many people still harvest Crab Apples for food today.

Crab Apple flower.

Cattail runners and Crab Apples for roasting.

Because the Crab Apple tree is so similar to an Apple tree, you can **graft**, or attach, the branch of a regular Apple variety like a Gala or a Red Delicious to a Crab Apple, and it will grow. This is helpful if you want to grow a fruit tree in a wet place.

Ellianna looks at raccoon tracks.

IMPORTANT NOTE

Raccoon scat can have harmful parasites in it, so while I encourage you to have a good look at it, do so with a stick so that you aren't breathing in the fumes! And while it might sound weird to look at something else's poop, it is actually very cool; you can tell what the animal has eaten and where it has been.

Pacific Crab Apple

Try This!
. . . .

RACCOON TRACKING

In the fall, Crab Apple skins can be easily spotted in raccoon scat. Raccoon tracks are easy to see in the mud or the soft sand of a beach. Raccoons often like to poop on top of fallen logs. If you come across some raccoon scat with Crab Apple skins in it, look around, and you will probably find a Crab Apple tree not too far away. Raccoons like to walk on the side of creek beds, as this is a great place to get water to drink and yummy things to eat like crabs, crayfish and slugs. With five long toes, raccoon tracks are very distinct, and very cute. See how far you can follow the trail of the raccoon. How long ago do you think it passed by? Can you tell how fresh the tracks are? How about how fresh the scat is? Can you see anything else in the scat that might tell you what else the raccoon has been eating? This activity can also be done in the city, where raccoons are happy to live and eat fruit like Grapes, Apples and Blackberries from people's yards.

The hand-like tracks of a Raccoon.

Harvesting Tip
. . . .

If you are patient and wait until the first frost, Crab Apples make a great snack right off the tree.

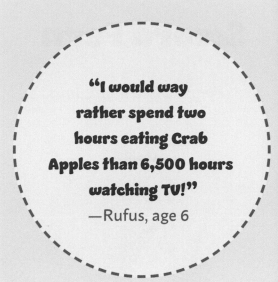

"I would way rather spend two hours eating Crab Apples than 6,500 hours watching TV!"
—Rufus, age 6

One-Minute Mystery
. . . .

I was walking along the edge of an **estuary** when I noticed that there were still old fence posts around from the days farmers kept their cows there. Then I noticed that there was a Crab Apple tree growing right next to every fence post. Why?

ANSWER: A bird who had eaten a Crab Apple had sat on the fence post and pooped out a Crab Apple seed. The seed then grew into a tree.

Sword Fern

Polystichum munitum

Guild: Red Cedar, Bigleaf Maple, Douglas Fir, Salal

Description

Sword Fern got its name from the shape of its leaves. When you look closely, you can see that the individual leaves on each frond are shaped like a tiny sword with a hilt. Sword Fern is abundant and evergreen in our area in moist woods.

Cool Facts about Sword Fern

Although ferns are plants, they are different from other plants, because they don't reproduce from seed. Instead they have spores, which send out a dust-like cloud. Walking through a forest of Sword Ferns in late summer, you can get covered by the soft brown pollen from the Fern's spores. You can see the spores on the underside of their leaves in little round groupings called sori.

Sword Fern.

Try This!

. . . .

PALA-PALA GAME

According to the entry on Sword Fern in *Plants of Coastal British Columbia*, for thousands of years, kids on the Coast have played in the Sword Ferns. They invented a game called the pala-pala game, and now you too can play this old game. All you do is see how many Fern leaves you can pick off the frond in one single breath while saying "pala" with each one. This game was so common among the Indigenous children of the Coast that the Sword Fern was known as the "pala-pala" plant.

> **"I think these would make perfect swords for a mouse!"**
> —Maya, age 7, holding up a Sword Fern frond

Maya plays the pala-pala game.

Katrina Rainoshek

Sword Fern   147

Thistle

Canada Thistle
Cirsium arvense

Bull Thistle
Cirsium vulgare

Edible Thistle
Cirsium edule

Guild: Wild Carrot, Burdock, Curly Dock, Yarrow, grasses

Description

A Thistle is hard to miss, especially if you are walking barefoot through a field in summer! With their spiky leaves and bristly pink-to-purple flowers, Thistles stand out in the grassy pastures, garden edges, roadsides and clearings where they like to grow. When they go to seed, their silky white fluff floats along and quickly spreads the seed to grow new Thistles. Thistles are in the Aster family.

Cool Facts about Thistle

The Thistle is the emblem of Scotland. Some say the reason for this dates all the way back to the eighth century, when the Norse army was invading Scotland. The Norse soldiers were sneaking up on the sleeping Scottish army when one of the Norse soldiers stepped on a thistle and yelled so loud it woke up the sleeping Scots, who were then able to fight off the Norse.

Bull Thistle.

Nibble This!

All Thistles are edible. We suggest wearing a glove when harvesting them to avoid the prickles, but if you don't have a glove, you can wrap a shirt or bandana around your hand. Use your digging stick to dig up the roots, and include them in your wild root roast. Or cut the Thistle stem at the ground, use a rock to scrape off the spikes and then peel the stem and eat it like celery. The fleshy middle vein, or midrib, in the leaves can also be peeled and eaten. Use a rock to pound off the spikes on the leaves, then tear away the leaf, leaving just the midrib to eat.

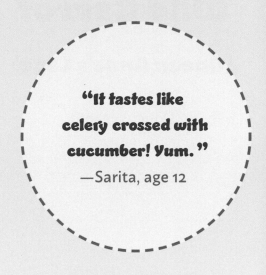

"It tastes like celery crossed with cucumber! Yum."
—Sarita, age 12

Preparing a Thistle leaf to eat.

Wild Carrot
(Queen Anne's Lace)

Daucus carota

CAUTION: When harvesting Wild Carrot, be sure not to confuse it with Poison Hemlock or Water Hemlock, which are in the same family but are deadly poisonous.

Guild: Yarrow, Sticky Gumweed, Pearly Everlasting, Thistle, Curly Dock

Description

Wild Carrot is also known as Queen Anne's Lace, because its frilly round white umbels of flowers look like lace. In the centre of most of the flowers is one small dark-red flower, thought to be the blood from Queen Anne's head being chopped off. Yikes! This plant was introduced from Europe and is now found all over North America in open fields, in meadows, along roadsides and in clearings. Before it flowers, its hairy leaves are long, green and feathery like a garden carrot. The root of Wild Carrot is not orange, though; it is creamy white, long and narrow.

Wild Carrot.

Nibble This!
. . . .

WILD ROOT ROAST

Supplies needed:

- digging stick or small shovel
- wild roots
- a campfire or oven
- tin foil
- oven mitt
- salt and butter (optional)

"They don't exactly taste as good as regular carrots, but they are kind of sweet once they are roasted."
—Mae, age 7

Mae harvests Wild Carrot with an Oceanspray digging stick.

There are so many wild foods to eat outside when you know where to look. This is a great autumn or winter activity for a fire on the beach. Using your Oceanspray digging stick, gather the roots of Wild Carrot, Thistle and Dock. They are especially easy to dig in the sandy soils near a beach. Dust or wash the dirt off the roots, cut them into small pieces and then wrap them in three layers of tin foil. Add a cut-up potato if you like. Place the packages in the coals of a fire and let them roast for fifteen to twenty minutes, turning occasionally. Bring some salt along to sprinkle on them, or a bit of butter for a gourmet dining experience!

Above left: Wild Carrot and Indian Consumption plant roots for roasting.

Above right: Preparing wild roots to roast.

Harvesting Caution Tip

What plants are in the same family as Wild Carrot and are deadly poisonous? Poison Hemlock and Water Hemlock! So if you are harvesting Wild Carrot, please double-check with a knowledgeable adult before touching the plant. Luckily, they grow in very different places: Water and Poison Hemlock grow at the edge of fresh water, and Wild Carrot prefers meadows, dry soil and roadsides.

Autumn Scavenger Hunt

1. Collect five different types of deciduous leaves.
2. Arrange your leaves from red to green.
3. Find a plant that grows an edible root.
4. Can you find a plant that still has berries on it?
5. Find two plants that are native to the area and two plants that were introduced from Europe.
6. Can you find a tree that makes nuts or seeds?
7. Point to the south. This is the direction birds are headed on their migrations.
8. Find, but don't collect, one poisonous plant.
9. Look under a pile of leaves on the ground. Do you see any creatures?
10. Which deciduous tree has lost the most leaves?

What did Harriet find on this wet fall day? A shelter built with teamwork and deciduous leaves.

Winter

The short days of winter are often grey and rainy on the Coast. This is a time when plants rest or go **dormant**. Deciduous trees have lost their leaves. In late winter, when the days start to warm up but the nights are still cold, sap starts running in the trees. Reds and yellows come into the tips of the Willows, and we can see tiny buds forming on the ends of Maples, Huckleberries and Salmonberries. This is a great season for getting to know the evergreen trees in your area.

Red Cedar

Guild: Cedar, Arbutus, Salal, Oregon Grape, Red Huckleberry, Sword Fern

Douglas Fir.

Description

Even though Douglas Fir and Grand Fir are both called Fir trees and are in the Pine family, they are not both "true" Firs. The Latin name of Douglas Fir, *Pseudotsuga*, actually means "false Hemlock." Many people, adults included, have a hard time telling these two trees apart. Here is the trick: Douglas, the tree, does not like to comb his hair, so it is always messy. Have a look at the needles of this tree—they are pointing every which way, sticking out from the twig like uncombed hair. Grand Fir, on the other hand, is like a grandfather who always keeps his hair neatly combed. His needles are parted in the middle and combed out to the sides.

There are some other differences as well. Douglas Fir is more common than Grand Fir. From a distance, older Douglas Firs often have the top blown off or branches growing all over the place, like their needles. Grand Fir, who likes to stay neat, grows in a more orderly cone shape. The needles of the trees differ as well. If you look closely, you can see that the tip of the Douglas Fir needle is rounded, and the tip of the Grand Fir is indented. The cones of the Grand Fir grow standing up on its branches and don't drop to the ground, whereas Douglas Fir cones grow hanging down and drop to the ground in great numbers. When you look closely,

Fir

Douglas Fir
Pseudotsuga menziesii

Grand Fir or Balsam Fir
Abies grandis

Douglas Fir cones have mice hidden in them. Read the story below to find out why! People often mistakenly call Fir cones Pine cones. Once you see the difference, you can kindly correct them, and you will never call a Fir cone a Pine cone again!

Cool Facts about Fir

When Grand Fir trees are young, the bark gets many sap bubbles under it, which kids love to pop and get all sticky with. This sap can be used to make glue. The bark on both trees gets rough when they are old, and the Douglas Fir bark gets so thick it can withstand forest fires. In an old forest, you can often see the black scars of long-ago fires on the bark. Some trees can live up to 1,000 years! These old trees make great wildlife trees. When

Grand Fir.

Alexander nibbles on
Douglas Fir tips.

a limb is blown off, a hole is created, making homes for **cavity nesters** such as Owls, Chickadees and Wood Ducks. In May, when the Firs begin to grow for the year, the fresh tips are bright green. These are very tasty and can be eaten fresh off the tree, added to salads or dried for tea. They are very high in vitamin C.

Sometimes the wood of Fir trees can be full of sap or pitch. People will sometimes buy pitch wood at camping stores for lighting fires because the sap is so flammable. At Salix School, we often make our own pitch sticks for lighting campfires. With these, I have even been able to light a fire in a downpour!

The Story of the Fir Cone Mice

Lightning crashed and thunder boomed, then *BLAST!*, a jolt of lightning ignited the top of a dead Fir tree. Soon the blaze spread and the forest smoked. "Help!" cried Mouse, as she tried to scamper away from the flames. In a panic, she ran here and she ran there, looking for a safe place to hide from the fire. "Over here!" called the voice of Douglas Fir. "Scamper up my trunk and hide in my cones." So Mouse dashed up the thick bark of the Fir, knowing that it would withstand the heat of any fire. She ran out to the tip of a long branch and, quickly as she could, ducked her head under a scale of one of the cones hanging down from the branch. There, she found not only shelter from the fire as it raged by, but also enough food in the seeds of the cones that she could wait out the fire in safety.

Douglas Fir did not brush his hair.

To this day, if you look closely at the cones of the Douglas Fir, you can see Mouse's tail and hind feet sticking out from the layers of the cone. And still to this day, as a thank you to the Douglas Fir for saving her life during the forest fire, Mouse takes the seeds from the cones and buries them, planting new seeds to make future trees.

Finding pitch wood.

Katrina Rainoshek

One-Minute Mystery

. . . .

I was walking through the forest one day when I spied something strange. There was a mushroom in a Fir tree! Not growing out of the tree like a conk, but placed high up in the crook of a branch. As I looked around, I saw other mushrooms as well, placed higher than a human could reach in the crook of a branch. After looking around a little more, I found a clue as to who had put these mushrooms up in the trees. This was the clue: a pile of scales from many Fir cones and a hole in the base of an old stump about as big as I could fit my arm in...who dunnit?

ANSWER: Douglas, Grey and Red Squirrels live on the Coast and like to collect mushrooms for their winter food. They are known for carrying them up a tree and placing them in the crook of a branch where the mushroom will dry and can be saved for a winter food source. Smart, hey? The pile of Fir cone scales was a squirrel midden, essentially the waste left behind after a squirrel has eaten the seeds from the Fir cones. The small hole was one of many openings to the squirrel's home.

Guild: Nettle, Licorice Fern, Sword Fern, Alder

Maple

Bigleaf Maple
Acer macrophyllum

Vine Maple
Acer circinatum

Douglas Maple
Acer glabrum

Description

Three kinds of Maple grow on the Coast. Bigleaf Maples are called that for a reason: their leaves can be bigger than dinner plates! These deciduous trees can grow to be very large; when they are old, they are often covered with thick moss and Licorice Ferns. Their huge canopies shade large areas, and the thousands of leaves they drop every autumn make the soil underneath rich. Because Maples grow back easily either after being cut down or after a fire, we often see Maples with many trunks sprouting from one stump or base, making great climbing places or spots to build a tree house.

Vine Maple and Douglas Maple are much smaller than Bigleaf Maple. They can be difficult to tell apart. The main difference between them is their leaves. Vine Maple has leaves with seven to nine lobes, while Douglas Maple has leaves with three to five lobes. Vine Maple is uncommon on Vancouver Island but common on the mainland. It likes to grow in moist wet areas. Douglas Maple is found all over the Coast, from dry ridges to moist forest edges. All three Maples have winged seeds.

Bigleaf Maple blossom.

Cool Facts about Maple

In the spring, the blossoms of the Bigleaf Maple are abuzz with the sound of bees. These bright flowers are edible and are best eaten before they are fully open. You can pop them in your mouth as a snack or harvest some to steam like broccoli or add to a quiche.

The helicopter seeds, called samaras, are great fun to throw up into the air and watch twirl down to the ground. The seeds sprout easily and can be transplanted to a garden or an area needing more trees.

Never too cool to eat
Maple blossoms!

Bigleaf Maple leaf.

Douglas Maple leaf.

MAKE YOUR OWN MAPLE SYRUP

Supplies needed:

- middle-aged Bigleaf Maple tree
- clean bucket
- hammer and 3″ nail
- drill with ½″ to 1″ bit
- spigot or clean ½″ to 1″ piping
- large pot
- wood stove, campfire, camp stove or home stove

Do you like Maple syrup? I sure do! Did you know you can make Maple syrup from our local Bigleaf Maple? Although it has less sugar in its sap than its Eastern cousin, the Sugar Maple, Bigleaf Maple makes very good syrup.

Gathering the sap is best done in late winter when the nights are cold—below freezing—and the days just above freezing. This ensures that the sap will be running up and down the tree. You will need to buy some

> "We made snow taffy with our maple syrup, and it was the most delicious thing I had ever tasted."
> —Stella, age 7

Stella and Tom check the Maple sap bucket. Katrina Rainoshek

Maple   **161**

In Japanese, the word *momijigari* means "Maple leaf hunting," and it is an activity that people still do today. This autumn, go out and do your own *momijigari* by finding as many beautiful leaves as you can!

spigots, which you can find online or at your local hardware store. You can also make some by bending tin pie plates into little tubes. With the help of an adult, drill a hole about half an inch wide into the trunk of a mid-sized tree whose bark is not yet thick like that of an old tree. The hole will not hurt the tree. Insert your spigot into the hole. Hammer a nail below the hole on which to hang a clean bucket in the evening. When the sap is running freely, check your bucket midday to see how much Maple sap you have gathered. This Maple water is delicious to drink fresh from the tree. To make it into syrup, the sap needs to be boiled down. The best way to do this is to put it in a stainless-steel pot on top of your wood stove, if you have one. Otherwise, you can do it on your kitchen stove, on a camp stove outside or by hanging it over an open fire outside. Turning the Maple water into syrup takes patience. It takes 10 litres of sap to make 100 millilitres of syrup...but it's worth it!

Guild: Douglas Fir, Arbutus; especially on southwest-facing slopes

Description

To the untrained eye, Oregon Grape can be confused with a small Holly bush. Both have sharp, waxy leaves of a similar size. But the similarities end there. The leaves of Holly are scalloped, darker green, glossy and shiny. Oregon Grape leaves are a duller green and do not have such deep scallops. The stems of the leaves are usually reddish and thin. In the spring, Oregon Grape makes clusters of very sweet-smelling small yellow flowers in the centre of the plant. These turn into dusty blue berries in midsummer and when ripe have a pleasant tartness when eaten in small quantities. The stems of the plant are woody, and when you scrape them with your fingernail or knife, they show a bright-yellow colour.

Oregon Grape.

Oregon Grape

Dull Oregon Grape
Mahonia nervosa

Tall Oregon Grape
Mahonia aquifolium

Oregon Grape berries.

Cutting up Oregon Grape root to show the yellow inside.
Katrina Rainoshek

Nibble This!
. . . .

In May, the fresh young leaves of Oregon Grape make a favourite snack for kids as they pass by. When the berries are dark dusty blue, they offer a tart but yummy treat.

"**Make sure you eat the berries when they are actually ripe. Otherwise, they are too bitter.**" —Zaylia, age 7

Cool Facts about Oregon Grape

Oregon Grape spreads by runners, long roots that spread across the ground just under the soil. These roots are bright yellow and contain a potent substance called berberine that is used as a powerful medicine against bacterial, viral and fungal infections. If you make a tea with them, it will become light yellow. The tea is also great for fighting colds, flus and runny noses. You can also use the tea as a wash for rashes and wounds.

Guild: Douglas Fir, Grand Fir, Hemlock, Spruce, Pine, Bigleaf Maple

Usnea.

Description

Usnea is a **lichen** that looks like long strands of hair. It is pale grey-green and has a rough texture. There are other similar-looking lichens. To tell them apart, gently pull on a strand of *Usnea*. There you will find a stretchy cord in the middle. *Usnea* grows draped from the branches of old trees.

Cool Facts about *Usnea*

Usnea grows only in healthy forests. When you see *Usnea* on trees, you know that the air of the forest is clean and that the forest is old. *Usnea* used to be widespread in northern forests, but there are now many places where it does not grow because of air pollution and logging. *Usnea* is a lichen, and a lichen is like two creatures in one. It is part fungi, which means "mushroom," and part **algae**. The fungi make a thick armour to protect the algae on the inside. The algae's job is to use the sun for photosynthesis. *Usnea* is used as a very strong medicine for colds, flus, infections and lung problems.

Old Man's Beard

Blood-Spattered Beard (!)
Usnea wirthii

Methuselah's Beard
Usnea longissima

(I just call it *Usnea*.)

Hey, you aren't an old man—
but nice old man's beard!

Try This!
. . . .

HEALTHY FOREST INQUIRY

Have you walked in a forest where *Usnea* grows? What did it feel like? Have you walked in forests where there is no *Usnea*? How were these forests different? What does a forest need to be healthy?

I once had a woman come to me with an infected Spider bite. She had gone to a few doctors and even taken antibiotics, but none of them cured the infection. I showed her how to make a tea from *Usnea*. She used it as a wash and as a drink, and within a week her infection had healed up!

Harvesting Tip
. . . .

Never pick *Usnea* off a tree where it is growing, as it takes a long time to grow. The best time to gather *Usnea* is after a big windstorm, when it is blown down out of the trees. It will dry easily in a basket and can be kept in a bag or jar for tea. This tea can be used for colds and flus and as a powerful wash for healing Brown Recluse Spider bites. I use a lot of *Usnea* medicine to help people heal from respiratory infections, so I go out walking after storms a lot to gather it.

Guild: Maple, Salmonberry, Sword Fern, Willow, Cottonwood

Alder.

Description

Alder is the most common deciduous tree growing on the Coast. At first glance, it can be confused with Cascara, Cottonwood, Dogwood or even young Maples in the winter. These trees all have similar white-, grey- and black-streaked bark, often with patches of green lichen. Alder leaves are toothed, while Cascara, Cottonwood and Dogwood leaf margins are smooth. Alder, along with Oak, is one of the last deciduous trees to drop its leaves in the fall. Preferring to grow in moist soil with access to sunlight, Alder can be found by streams and lakes, in moist woods and clear-cuts, and on old logging roads. It often grows in stands. Being a very soft tree easily taken over by rot, Alder usually lives to be only seventy years old.

Red Alder

Alnus rubra

Cool Facts about Alder

Alder is what is called a **pioneer tree** because it is often one of the first species to grow after an area has been clear-cut or bulldozed. It also grows on old roads. By making shade and soil with its leaves, Alder creates areas where other plants can begin to grow. Alder takes nitrogen out of the air and releases it into the soil. The inner bark of Alder can be eaten in the spring, similar to Pine, and the twigs and bark have a long history as an important medicine.

A Pacific Tree Frog on an Alder leaf.

> "I was sure that the Maple twig was an Alder twig until I remembered that Maple buds are opposite each other and Alder are alternate. Once you figure out the patterns, it is so much easier to tell the difference!"
> —Alexander, age 9

Try This!

GUESS THIS BUD

Winter is a great time to practise your plant identification skills. During the rest of the year there are leaves or flowers to give you clues as to what plant you are looking at. In winter we have an extra challenge in telling who is who without these. Choose three to five twigs from various deciduous trees. Look closely at each one. What do the buds look like? Do they have catkins? What pattern is the bark? Do the buds smell? Are they sticky? Give the twigs to your friend, parent or instructor and have them guess which twig belongs to which tree. Now it's your turn. Can you guess three or four twigs given to you? Once you do this a few times, you will never mix up Alder with Cascara or Dogwood again!

Guess the twig! Katrina Rainoshek

168 Red Alder

Red Flowering Currant after a rain.

Guild:

Oceanspray, Douglas Fir, Arbutus, Oak, Red Huckleberry, Honeysuckle

Red Flowering Currant.

Red Flowering Currant

Ribes sanguineum

"Whoa, Red Flowering Currant really does look like a fountain of blood...if I use my imagination."
—Milliano, age 10

Description

For most of the year, Red Flowering Currant (or RFC, as plant geeks like me call it) goes unnoticed. Then early spring comes along, and you might say, "Whoa, where did those bright-red flowers come from?!" This is the best part of the RFC. Being in the currant family means that RFC has small, alternate, deciduous, three-lobed leaves. The flowers are dark pinkish-red and look like little clusters of trumpets up close. In the summer, the flowers turn into small grey-blue berries that are edible, but sour. RFC likes to grow from old stumps, in dry clearings or wherever a bird poops out a seed.

Cool Facts about Red Flowering Currant

RFC's Latin name, *sanguineum*, means "bloody," referring to the flowers, which to some minds might look like a fountain of blood! The bright colour of RFC attracts hummingbirds and bees, and because it is an early bloomer, it is an important source of nectar on the cold days of early spring.

MAKE MORE RED FLOWERING CURRANTS

Supplies needed:

- Red Flowering Currant bush in the winter
- hand pruners
- plant pot
- potting soil
- rooting hormone (optional)

> Look for Red Flowering Currants under power lines where birds poop out the seeds.

Plants in the currant family are easily **propagated**. Pay attention to where you see a many-stemmed RFC when it blooms in the spring. Go back anytime between late November and early January with a pair of hand pruners, and cut one or two of the long straight branches at their base. You can either dip the bottom of the cuttings in a bit of rooting hormone first or just stick them in a planter pot full of soil so that six inches of the base of the cutting are covered. You can also plant them directly in the ground, as long as you remember to give them a little water the first year. It may take them a few years to flower, but be patient. The bees and the hummingbirds will thank you.

Left: Breah makes a Red Flowering Currant cutting. Katrina Rainoshek

Right: Red Flowering Currant cuttings in their pot. Katrina Rainoshek

Guild: Fir, Cedar, Salmonberry, Sword Fern, Skunk Cabbage

Sitka Spruce.

Description

Sitka Spruce is an evergreen tree that likes to grow in rich, moist areas, like the edges of rivers, streams and marshes. You can also get to know them by their blue-green needles, their puzzle-piece-like bark when they are old and their cones, whose thin scales turn a light brown when they fall to the ground.

Cool Facts about Spruce

The largest Sitka Spruce is 84 metres (275 feet) tall. That is as tall as the Statue of Liberty! The trunk of the tree is 4.5 metres (15 feet) wide, maybe as wide as your living room.

Sitka Spruce

Picea sitchensis

The quickest way to know you have met a Spruce tree is to shake hands with it. Its sharp needles will poke into your hands. "Never shake hands with a spruce," they say.

A humongous Sitka Spruce.

Talk about old growth!

A tree this big takes a long time to grow. Can you imagine what the world was like 800 years ago? That was around the year 1200. There were thriving Indigenous cultures on the Coast, and no Spanish or English ships had arrived here yet. Kublai Khan was invading China, and the Crusades were taking place in Europe. Can you imagine being alive that long? You could have great-great-great-great-great-great-great-great-great-great-grandchildren! Because these trees can live so long, they become the home of many plants and animals, like an old-growth skyscraper. Moss grows on the thick branches, offering a soft place for the endangered Marbled Murrelet to build its nest. Because Spruce trees have such dense, thick branches, they make great places for birds and animals to hide in the cold wet weather on the Coast. The Haida people are renowned for making baskets from the roots of the Spruce tree so tightly woven that they can hold water. Some people like to chew the sap from Spruce trees—the original chewing gum!

Try This!
· · · · · · · · · ·

MEET A TREE

This group activity is great for getting to know trees—and our many senses—in a deep way. Get into pairs. One person is blindfolded, and their partner's job is to walk them carefully, but not in a straight line, to a tree. There, the blindfolded person "meets" the tree, using all their senses except sight. They can feel the bark, the branches, the shape of the leaves. Have them smell the sap or the buds and taste the needles or the fruits. And have them listen to the tree itself and the birds in its branches. Now lead the blindfolded person back a different way to the starting point. Remove their blindfold and ask them to find their tree! This is a great time to have the participants draw their tree, developing their sense of sight. This tree will probably make an impression on the person and be remembered for a long time.

Supplies needed:
- trees
- bandana
- a partner

Milliano "meets" a tree.

A blindfolded walk.

Sitka Spruce   **173**

Western Hemlock.

Guild: Douglas Fir, Grand Fir, Red Cedar, Salal; rich, moist forests

Western Hemlock

Tsuga heterophylla

Description

Hemlock has the shortest needles of all the evergreen trees on the coast. It also has small cones. The needles form a dense, feathery pattern that doesn't let very much light pass through to the forest floor. This means not much grows under the Hemlock, except maybe more Hemlock, which doesn't mind growing in the shade. Hemlocks are easy to spot, because the very top of the tree droops over to one side.

Cool Facts about Hemlock

Hemlocks have a lot of **tannins** in them. These make a reddish colour when the wood or branches are soaked in water. People use this to tan deer hides for making leather. People on the Coast also use this dye to colour basket materials and wool, and they even used it as makeup. The inner bark of Hemlock trees can be eaten like Pine.

Saving the Old-Growth Forest

It was nearing my eighteenth birthday when I learned of an old-growth forest that was due to be logged. A group of people had been trying to stop the ancient trees from being cut down, but the government and the logging company were not listening. I felt sad and angry that trees older than any human were being cut down to make lumber or, even worse, toilet paper. These forests were home to rare animals like the Northern Goshawk, a large, fierce raptor, and the Wolverine, an elusive, ferocious hunter in the Weasel family. Didn't the government realize that we needed these old forests to help balance out the effects of the carbon emissions that cause climate change? Didn't they realize that these forests, with trees over 800 years old, are so rare that there are only 2 percent of them left? Cutting them down is like killing Blue Whales! We realized that asking the government and the logging companies to stop cutting old-growth forests wasn't working. They didn't seem to care that it was our future, not theirs. All they cared about was making money.

So I got together with a group of friends, and we got ourselves organized. With people who knew what to do, we went to this beautiful forest and made it our home for a little while. We set up a kitchen and we built a few trails so that people could come and see how special these forests are. Sadly, the day the logging was to begin was fast approaching. All the talks and the marches in the city hadn't worked. By now, we had made friends with this old forest. We watched birds swoop between the branches. We swam in the cold river. We ate the dark Black Huckleberries until our fingers turned blue. What were we going to do? When you love something or someone, you can't stand to watch it get hurt.

After much thought, we decided we would move into the trees! Surely they couldn't cut the forest down if we

Esme and Breah take a stand for their future.

It is common to see Hemlock trees that are dying. There are diseases that are causing their needles to drop off and their roots and trunks to rot. One winter a windstorm blew a very large Hemlock down, missing our house by only 1 metre (3 feet). Phew! Its needles were still green, but the whole inside of the trunk was hollowed out by rot.

lived in the trees! With climbing ropes and harnesses, platforms and pulleys, we made little houses way up high in the branches of the trees. I felt like a bird, way up there, 53 metres (175 feet) off the ground. As I lay cozy in my sleeping bag, I would watch as the sun made feathery shadows through the Hemlock branches. Pine Siskins would visit me for some seeds from my trail mix. And for a while, the forest we loved was safe. No one could figure out how to get us down, and they couldn't cut the trees around us, because we might get hurt.

Then, on the morning of my eighteenth birthday, I heard a sound coming from the sky that wasn't a bird. It was a helicopter that had come to take us out of our trees. "Goodbye," I whispered to the feathery fronds of the Hemlock. "Goodbye," I called to Mouse, who had stolen my peanuts so high up in the tree. "Goodbye, beautiful old forest. I tried to save you, and that was the best I could do." I cried as I was taken away from my treetop home.

Try This!

. . . .

WHO AM I?

Write out the names of local plants on pieces of masking tape, enough so that every person gets at least one. For the advanced version, use Latin names. Each person gets a piece of tape with a plant name stuck to their forehead without them seeing what is written on it. Using yes-or-no questions, have the players ask each other questions to try to find out which plant they are. For example: "Am I a tree with needles? Do I have small cones? Do I like to grow in sunny places?" This is a great way to encourage the skill of question asking, and also of having the players identify with a specific plant and get to know it.

Supplies needed:
* masking tape
* pen
* four to twenty players

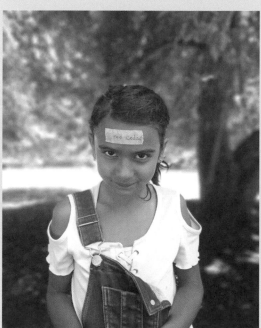

Margret plays "Who am I?"

Isabella and Breah in
the "Who am I?" game.

Western Hemlock   **177**

Western Red Cedar

Thuja plicata

Western Red Cedar.

Guild: Douglas Fir, Hemlock, Grand Fir, Alder, Sword Fern, Salmonberry

Description

Western Red Cedar is an evergreen tree that likes to grow in moist, shady forests. It has swooping branches with feathery fronds and small brown cones. The bark of the Red Cedar is grey and peels off in long strips. Very old trees often have wide **buttressed** trunks that flare out at the base to give the huge trees more support. Where the roots of the Red Cedar come to the ground, you can see the dark-red colour that gives the tree its name. Red Cedar is easily confused with Yellow Cedar, which usually grows at a higher **elevation** than Red Cedar. The fronds of the Yellow Cedar hang straight down, while the Red Cedar's fronds swoop up. If you rub your hand backward along the Yellow Cedar, the fronds are sharp, whereas Red Cedar fronds are soft. Red Cedar has a rich sweet smell, but Yellow Cedar smells musty. Old-growth Cedar trees can get up to 60 metres (200 feet) tall, or as high as four school buses standing end on end. Old Cedars that have been hollowed out from fire or rot make important places for Black Bears to den. If you have never seen an old-growth Cedar, encourage the adults in

> I have seen some Cedars so big that it took eleven kids to get their arms around!

your life to take you on a trip to see them. They are like the Blue Whales of the land: rare, enormous and important.

Cool Facts about Red Cedar

Western Red Cedar is called the Tree of Life by the Indigenous cultures on the Coast. In fact, this tree is what shaped much of the culture here before Europeans came. Can you imagine a tree big enough to make a canoe that can fit twenty people? Or a tree big enough to make a whole longhouse out of? Clothes, blankets, hats, containers, cradles, paddles, baskets, dishes, arrows, furniture, totem poles, medicine and many more things are made from Cedar, all without having to cut down the tree. Before people had metal tools, they used wedges made from the hard wood of Yew trees or from antlers to split out sections of the tree. The wood of Red Cedar is very rot-resistant, which makes it great for houses and canoes. In fact, it is so rot-resistant that it can take a fallen Red Cedar up to 600 years to fully break down and turn back into the forest floor.

How many kids can fit inside one old-growth Western Red Cedar?

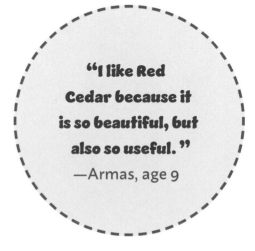

"I like Red Cedar because it is so beautiful, but also so useful."
—Armas, age 9

If you are ever caught without soap after using the bathroom in the woods, you can rub your hands over the fronds of Cedar. The oils in the Cedar are antiseptic, like hand sanitizer. It is still a good idea to wash your hands well when you do find some soap and water.

. . . .

MAKE YOUR OWN TINDER

The inner bark of Cedar makes great tinder, which, along with some pitch wood, will get a fire going in any weather. Find an older Cedar tree where some of the strips of bark are hanging a bit loose from the trunk. Notice what direction the wind and rain come from. Notice if one side of the tree is wet and the other dry. Now choose a dry place to pull off a strip of bark about as long as your forearm. The underside of the bark has a reddish-brown colour and is often dry. This red inner bark is what makes the tinder. With the edge of a stone, a shell or your knife, rub the soft inner bark off the thick grey outer bark. Then work the soft bark into smaller and smaller pieces until you have a fluffy pile of tinder. This can be put in your pocket to help it dry out even more until you light your fire. If you do this at the beginning of the day and have your fire in the afternoon, your tinder should be nice and dry. Remember, always ask an adult before you light a fire, and check the local rules about campfires.

Left top: Making tinder with the inner bark of Cedar.

Left bottom: **Margret makes Cedar tinder.** Katrina Rainoshek

Guild: Maidenhair Fern, Goat's Beard, Cottonwood, Cedar, Fir; creeksides, riversides

Western Yew or Pacific Yew

Taxus brevifolia

Description

Yew trees are evergreen and are not to be confused with *ewes* (female sheep) or *you*, who is reading this book. Yews are lovely and uncommon trees. At first they can be hard to spot, because they look so similar to Hemlock and Fir trees. You will only find them growing near the water or in very moist, healthy forests. Although Yew trees don't grow higher than a one-storey house, they look very old, covered in a green cape of moss. Their bark is reddish and peeling. Some trees have orangey-red berries. The cones of Yew are very hard to spot since they are small and hidden on the underside of the branch.

Pacific Yew.

Cool Facts about Yew

The wood of the Yew is very hard, so it was the best wood for making tools in the past. Even today, people still make tools and bows (but not arrows; see Oceanspray for arrows) from this wood if they can find it. Another thing that is

Yew trees can change their gender! Male Yew trees can turn themselves into female trees if there are not enough female trees around to be pollinated by the male trees.

made from the Yew tree is a strong medicine for cancer. The berries of this tree are poisonous, though, so don't eat them. Yew trees have either female or male cones, so two trees are needed to pollinate each other.

A very old Yew tree.

MAGIC WANDS

Making magic wands is fun for all ages. Take some time to wander and find just the right stick. A gnarled twig of a Yew tree, the straight shoot of a Nootka Rose, a patterned old beaver chew or a smooth polished piece of driftwood. Keep your eyes open for feathers, shells and other special things to tie onto your wand. Bring string, ribbon, beads and scissors to enhance your creation. When your wand is finished, cast some spells!

Supplies needed:
- small saw or hand pruners for cutting wands
- string, ribbons
- scissors

MAGIC SPELLS

Have you ever said the Latin names of plants out loud? Doesn't *Drosera rotundifolia!* sound like a spell from Harry Potter? Especially with an exclamation mark at the end. Perhaps it turns you into a fly, cures warts or even makes someone fall in love with you. Can you think of any other Latin name magic spells? What about *Asarum caudatum*, which is the Latin name for Wild Ginger? Maybe this spell makes you hot all over, turns your enemies into slugs or cures tummy aches. But be careful—follow the rule all magic makers have to follow, which is "Do unto others as you would have done unto you!"

Making magic with our newly carved magic wands.

Western Yew   **183**

Pine

Western White Pine
Pinus monticola

Shore Pine
Pinus contorta

Shore Pine.

Guild:

White Pine: Salal, Oregon Grape, Douglas Fir; ridge tops, lakeshores, forest edges

Shore Pine: Arbutus, Manzanita, Salal; sandy or rocky soils, ocean shores

Description

Pine trees have the longest needles of the Coastal evergreen trees. Western White Pine has longer needles than Shore Pine. The needles of White Pine are in groups of five, whereas the needles of the Shore Pine grow in groups of two. You can see this when you look up close at the branch where the needles grow. The cones of both of these Pine trees are also a good way to tell them apart. White Pine cones can grow to be a foot long and look like what you think of when you hear "Pine cone." Shore Pines have smaller cones that are kind of lumpy and have a sharp tip on the end of each scale. White Pines usually grow tall and straight. Shore Pines, like their name suggests, often grow right by the ocean shore on rocky bluffs and get twisted by the wind. That is why their Latin name is *contorta*, which means "twisted." When Shore Pine grows away from the shore, up in the hills or bluffs, it is straight-trunked and doesn't grow higher than 6 metres (20 feet) tall.

Cool Facts about Pine

Shore Pine sometimes grows in bogs, places where there is not much soil. Because of this, it grows very slowly, becoming bonsai trees only 30 centimetres (1 foot) tall but 100 years old!

The inner bark of Pine trees can be eaten. In fact, it is quite sweet, and the texture is a bit like chewing gum crossed with noodles. The sap is also sweet and can be collected to cook down into glue for sealing boats and making tools. The sap helps heal cuts just by putting it right on the wound.

Western White Pine.

"When I find a ball of Pine sap, I like to chew it like chewing gum!"
—Tosh, age 12

Who will come eat the seeds at this Pine cone bird feeder?

WESTERN WHITE PINE CONE BIRD FEEDERS

Supplies needed:
- large Pine cones
- peanut butter or lard
- birdseed
- a tray or baking pan
- string

Many birds like to eat the seeds from inside Pine cones. Now you can give them another treat. Once the cones fall to the ground, the birds are usually done with them. Collect a few cones. Tie a string around one end. Then you can roll the cones in either peanut butter or suet, or use a butter knife to smear it on and under the scales. On a baking tray, pour out some birdseed and then roll your sticky cone in it, shaking off the extra when you are done. Hang the cones in the trees in your yard so you can enjoy the feeding flocks of Winter Juncos, Nuthatches, Chickadees and Pine Siskins.

Yerba Buena.

Guild: Oregon Grape, Wild Strawberry, Douglas Fir, Arbutus, Twinflower

Yerba Buena

Satureja douglasii

Description

The small vine-like Yerba Buena plant often forms a large mat in sunny, dry places. Its square stem, a sure sign that it is in the Mint family, is slightly woody, with opposite leaves that are smooth and evenly spaced. In the summer it grows small trumpet-shaped white flowers and keeps its leaves on all winter. The sweet, spicy, lemony smell of Yerba Buena is unmistakable when crushed by our feet or rubbed between our fingers.

Yerba Buena means "good herb" in Spanish and was named so by early Spanish sailors on the Coast.

TEA TIME

Supplies needed:

- Yerba Buena
- scissors or a knife for harvesting
- campfire or camp stove
- kettle that can go on a fire
- tin cups
- honey (optional)

Yerba Buena makes delicious tea. It can be picked any time of year, which makes it a nice addition to a wintertime fireside tea. Use a knife or scissors to snip the Yerba Buena from the ends of its spreading stems.

You can bunch the plants together at their bases and tie them with string or an elastic band and hang them to dry. Once dry, strip off the leaves and store them in an airtight jar or bag somewhere cool and dark. It is the volatile oils in

Making winter tea.

"This is the best tea ever! I think the Yerba Buena really makes it good."
—Bella, age 11, as she sipped her hot tea around our campfire.

188 Yerba Buena

these plants that give them their flavour and make them great for colds, flus and stomach aches.

Have you ever had tea made over a campfire? This is one of our school's winter highlights. Bring an old kettle (we call ours "The Royal Kettle") especially for the occasion. What wild tea ingredients do you think you might find on a cold December day? Some things I add are Grand Fir and Hemlock needles, Blackberry and Strawberry leaves, Oregon Grape root and Yerba Buena. With an adult's help, put the plants you have gathered into your kettle or teapot.

To keep the volatile oils in when you make the tea, pour boiling water over the plants and then cover with a lid before you let the tea steep for fifteen minutes. Be careful when you pour your tea; it will be hot! Strain and drink a warm cup of wild tea. Yum!

Bella carving with winter tea at the beach.

Making winter tea.

Yerba Buena **189**

Winter Twig Quiz

Here are thirteen twigs from local deciduous trees. Can you figure out which one is which? The answers are below.

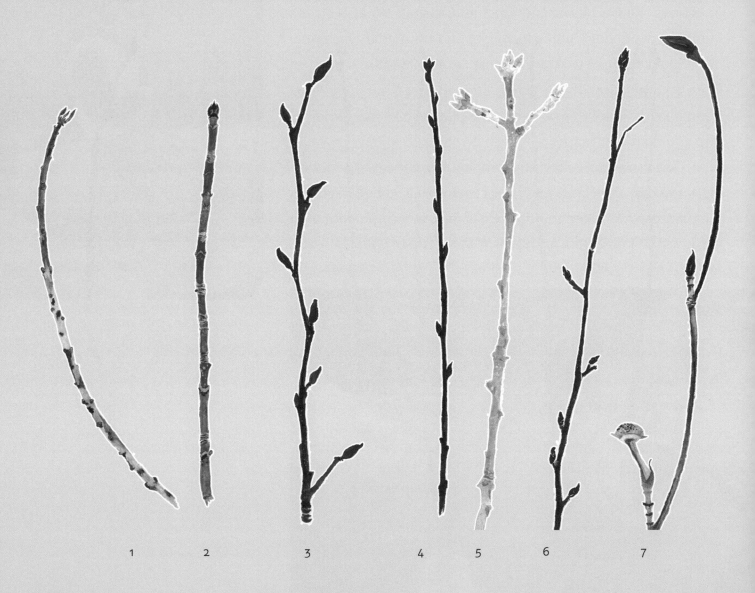

1 2 3 4 5 6 7

190

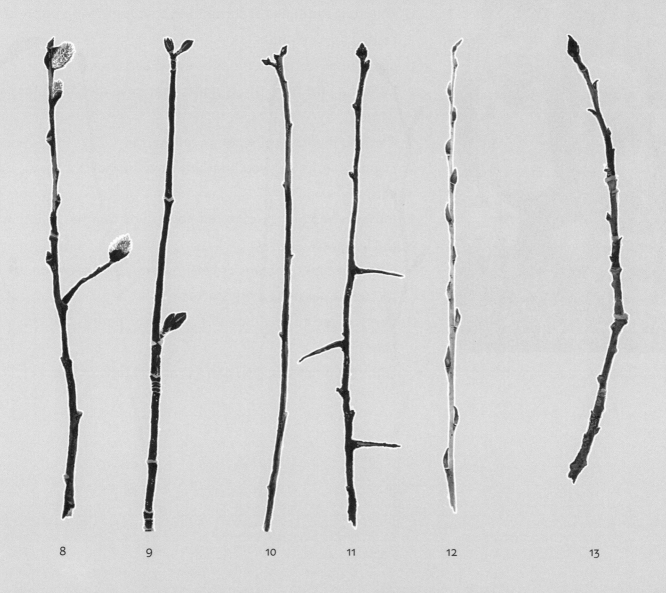

ANSWERS: 1. Cascara; 2. Bigleaf Maple; 3. Alder; 4. Bitter Cherry; 5. Garry Oak; 6. Saskatoon; 7. Pacific Flowering Dogwood; 8. Hooker's Willow; 9. Vine Maple; 10. Pacific Crab Apple; 11. Hawthorn; 12. Pacific Willow; 13. Trembling Aspen

8   9   10   11   12   13

Winter Scavenger Hunt

Who was having Fir cones for lunch?

1. Find three plants with thick or waxy leaves. Why do you think they grow like this?

2. Find four examples of something that is growing but is not technically a plant.

3. Collect four different types of evergreen cones.

4. Collect a part from three plants that have died back for the winter.

5. Can you find the tracks of an animal?

6. Listen quietly. Can you hear any birds? What are they eating?

7. Can you find any clues to tell how much rain has fallen in the last week?

8. Find two types of plant or tree material that could be used for dry tinder or as a fire starter.

9. Can you see any examples of an animal eating plants or cones?

10. Find one plant that you can eat at this time of year.

Tree Quiz

. . . .

1. Which tree makes clothes, medicine, houses, canoes, tools and baskets?
2. Is an Arbutus tree deciduous? How about an Alder? Or a Grand Fir?
3. True or false: Hemlock trees make large cones.
4. How do you know when you are shaking hands with a Spruce tree?
5. Which has longer needles: White Pine or Shore Pine?
6. Name two trees that make "catkins." What are catkins?
7. True or false: Alder leaves are "toothed."
8. Which two trees are easily confused: Crab Apple and Alder, Crab Apple and Hawthorn, or Crab Apple and Cottonwood?
9. Whose cone did Mouse hide under during a forest fire?
10. Which tree makes acorns and provides important habitat for rare plants and animals?
11. True or false: Hawthorn trees are related to Apples.
12. Which Fern likes to grow from the mossy trunks of old Bigleaf Maples?

Western White Pine.

ANSWERS: 1. Cedar; 2. Yes, yes, no; 3. False; 4. The needles are sharp; 5. White Pine. 6. Alder and Cottonwood have catkins, which are hanging strands of small flowers; 7. True; 8. Crab Apple and Hawthorn; 9. Douglas Fir; 10. Garry Oak; 11. True; 12. Licorice Fern

10

For Parents and Educators

Hello, parents, educators and other adults who care about the planet.

Although I began writing this book many years ago, the bulk of it was written in 2021, during the COVID-19 pandemic. Like all people, I was affected by the pandemic in many ways. As a mother, a clinical herbalist, an outdoor educator and an on-call paramedic, life has shifted from the "old normal" to the "new normal." But I am lucky to live on a small island on the west coast of Canada. Although "distanced," my family and I still live within a web of community and in a place where children play outdoors in all weather. We have vast areas to roam without busy traffic, fences or lockdown orders. Many children the world over are not so lucky. This book is for those children as much as it is for children who have access to places where wild plants grow.

We have all the statistics we need about children spending less time outside and too much time inside on a screen. Most of us know, even intuitively, that this is an issue that causes damage. Despite this, many parents and educators struggle with how to shift this balance, even as the world opens up again.

My suggestion is to start close to home. If you live in the city, find a park, empty lot or backyard to become your nature connection place. Plants are everywhere. So are birds, insects and animals. Many people tell themselves that they can't connect with nature unless they are in the "wilderness," but this doesn't need to be true. A Starling calls from the telephone wire, just as a Swainson's Thrush calls from the Salmonberry bush. A Cooper's Hawk is just as likely to swoop down and catch either bird by surprise. Raccoons cross my yard on the rural island I live on just as they will cross the sidewalk in front of a city house. Dandelions grow on lawns and in backyards all over the northern hemisphere. It matters less *where* you get outside than *that* you are getting outside. (That said, if you have the means, make sure you and your family experience the wonder of an old-growth forest before they are gone.)

Wilderness connections and outdoor activities are dominated by white, middle-class, able-bodied people, like me. While holding the awareness that not everyone has the time, energy, money or capacity to go into the wilderness, I encourage everyone to get outside in some way. You don't need fancy gear, or even a car. Find a park in your neighbourhood that is accessible. Join a group of families who go out together. Support each other by sharing rides, gear, ideas and kid care. Let's work together to break down the

It took the arms of seven kids to encircle this old-growth Douglas Fir!

Whose feather is this?

Katrina Rainoshek

race and class barriers that separate people from each other and from the world of the outdoors.

The future of this planet and all the species that live here depends on today's children connecting to where they live and with the other living beings there. Becoming attuned to nature and to one's senses brings higher levels of empathy, nourishes the nervous system and increases a feeling of connectedness rather than separation. These are qualities that encourage communication, community, self-confidence, trust and leadership. When a child, or an adult, has a relationship with a place and the creatures who live there, whether it is an abandoned lot, their backyard or an ancient rainforest, they care for it and become its steward.

In this time of climate chaos, social upheaval, class and racial division and increasing addiction to screens, reconnecting to nature is a high priority. My hope with this field guide is that through hands-on activities, children and adults alike will be able to go beyond just naming a plant or tree to developing a relationship with it. By eating, drinking and using materials from the world around us, we engage in reciprocity and experience the generosity of the earth. This in turn helps us feel at home in the outdoors, reminding us that the earth has always provided us with all our basic needs and that we must care for the earth in return.

This field guide is for children, youth and adults alike. Although I have included some technical language as a way of introducing the language of botany into our daily lives, most of the book is written to be accessible and interesting to people of all ages. Once again, it is the relationship with place and plants that has the impact, not whether a person can tell the difference between petals or bracts. With enough time, the science and the intuition merge to create a holistic way of knowing a plant.

Tips for Adults

Teaching nature connection to children is a bit of a misnomer. Without our meddling, children are inherently connected to nature. It is only through socialization that they become disconnected from nature. Perhaps we need a guide not on nature connection but on "how to not disconnect from nature in the first place!" Keeping this in mind, here are some ideas for how to encourage a deeper connection with the outdoors:

- Being outside is fun! Children need to be in their bodies, to move and to be in a state of wonder and play. If they are out of this habit, it may take some convincing and some modelling to help them remember how to play. Run, play tag, build faerie houses or forts, listen to the birds, get dirty. Join them in the fun.
- Have a regular, built-in practice in your home or classroom life that gives children unstructured time in unstructured places where spontaneous interactions with imagination, plants and creatures can happen.

Raincoats, a campfire and roasted apples make a rainy day so much fun!

Playing bat and moth.

- Model play, inquiry and connection. When outside with kids, engage. Find things that pique your interest, and share your enthusiasm. Look up things you don't know online or in field guides with the kids. Ask children what they think, what they notice, what they are surprised about.

- Asking questions rather than giving answers encourages deeper learning. When children have to find an answer themselves, they will then feel connected to the process of inquiry. Groups of children love the challenge of solving a problem together. Give them challenges that make them think beyond a surface answer.

- Interact with your surroundings. Show kids that it's okay to get dirty digging up roots. Crouch down to look closely at a flower. Munch some Miner's Lettuce. Collect some leaves. Be part of the world, because you are.

Tools, Supplies and Safety

One of the great parts of connecting with nature is that you don't need anything except yourself to do it. Your eyes, ears, hands, feet, mouth and heart are all the equipment you need. That said, there are a few things that can help further your connection and interaction with the world of plants. Here are some items I recommend and some supplies you will need to do some of the activities in this book.

Outdoor Gear

Quality rain gear allows all of us on this "wet" coast to enjoy every season even more. If you have the means, invest in rain boots that are comfortable to walk in and rain pants and a raincoat that actually keep you dry. Good gear is costly, and we don't all have the funds for it. Check out used gear swaps. Many communities are starting gear libraries where you can borrow outdoor gear. Check whether your community has one. If it doesn't, start one.

Knives

Kids love the agency of having their own knife. In my outdoor program, I start most kids with their own knife and teach them knife skills at age five, give or take. But not all kids. I have to see that they are ready. Some signs of knife readiness include:
- able to follow directions
- able to sit still
- able to do other projects, like crafts, that require manual dexterity and hand-eye coordination
- an interest in knife-associated skills, such as food preparation or whittling

At the nature school where I teach, I suggest fixed-blade knives like Mora knives, which have a well-fitted sheath.

Even with the warmth of a campfire, kids need many layers of winter clothes to stay warm and happy outdoors.

These are good for bushcraft applications like splitting pitch wood and cutting thick- or woody-stemmed plants. A folding knife with an easy lock, like an Opinel, is a good choice because it fits small hands and has a sensitive blade for carving and cutting food. Both of these knives are easy to handle and safe, and they lend themselves to being sharpened. Stay away from folding knives with no lock, like Swiss Army knives. Blades should be no more than four inches long. A knife is less likely to cut the user if it is well sharpened, which is a skill I teach once basic knife skills are met.

To begin teaching knife skills, I sit with the child one-on-one at first, demonstrating basic whittling, cutting away

Opinel knife.

from themselves, and determining which wood to choose. When I see safe knife use, children are allowed to use their knives in groups at carving time or during activities where knives are appropriate. All children must ask before they take out their knives and only when they are sitting down with a "blood bubble" around them. The blood bubble is a key to knife safety. This means checking with the knife user's outstretched arms that the area around them is safe and there is no one else in the "blood bubble." The knife must always be put away properly before the child stands up.

When a knife user accidentally cuts themself for the first time, I celebrate the consequence of tool use, clean and treat the cut with Yarrow or Plantain, apply a bandage and encourage the child to continue. Most knife cuts that happen when a child is learning to use a knife are minimal and safe if the knife is being used properly.

Other Sharp Tools

Small folding saws, light hatchets and hand pruners are useful tools for cutting staves, making kindling, cutting branches, snipping up roots for medicine and cutting saplings for structures. These are tools reserved for skilled hands; although some six-year-olds can use these tools with proper instruction and supervision, the tools are more often in the hands of a teenager or an adult. Any age is a great age to teach the empowerment that comes with tool use.

Making a feather stick.

Katrina Rainoshek

June learning carving.

Lighting the Douglas Fir pitch wood.

Katrina Rainoshek

Matches, Lighters, Flint and Steel and Ferro Rods
Not everyone lives in a place where making a fire outside is an option. For those for whom sitting around a campfire is a once-in-a-lifetime experience, it is often fondly remembered. Making tea from wild plants over a fire is one of my favourite activities to do in the winter. Find out which parks, beaches or recreation sites near you allow outdoor fires and when the local fire bans are so that you can share the wonderful experience of a campfire with kids!

There are many ways of lighting a fire when you are outside. I find the easiest method for children is with good-quality wooden matches, as long as a fire is built well, with dry tinder. Lighters are challenging, because they get

hot and have a tendency to burn the thumb. A flint and steel or ferro rod takes practice, but a fire lit with a spark from these is exciting. Small fluffy dry tinder is a must!

When working with fire, tie back long hair, roll up sleeves and remove puffy jackets. Children at my outdoor school are challenged to build their own fires but have to ask before they take out any matches or lighters. I encourage them to use as few matches as possible by handing out the matches instead of giving them the whole box. This ensures they are mastering their fire-making skills and not using the matches as tinder! Before they try lighting the fire, check that they are safe and that they have the proper materials at hand: dry tinder, small twigs and mid-sized pieces of wood as well as larger ones. "A fire is like a hungry baby," I tell them. "It wants to be fed a lot of small bites."

Snipping Oregon Grape root.

Katrina Rainoshek

Pen, Paper, Sketchbooks and Art Supplies

Drawing plants while actually sitting right next to them is an irreplaceable way to really see a plant. Not only might the artist see parts of the plant they never noticed before, but they can also convey the "feeling" of a plant, even if the drawing does not botanically represent it. Providing the

Chapter 10   **203**

Practising fire-starting skills.

Poet makes a map.

artists with their own sketchbooks and quality art supplies like pencils, pencil crayons, pastels and felt-tip markers enhances the experience. A small pocket-sized notebook is helpful for jotting down questions, observations, mysteries and leaf and plant sketches to look up later.

Magnifying Glass and Jewellers' Loupe

Jewellers' loupes, which fold up into a small case, can be easily carried on a cord around the neck, while magnifying glasses are a little bulkier. Both are great for bringing the world of the small into focus. Pollen anthers, iridescent beetle shells, leaf edges, feathers and millions of other finds become a whole new experience when seen up close.

Medicine-Making Supplies

- Small clean jars with tight-fitting lids can be kept out of the recycling, or you can purchase small canning jars. Baby food jars and washed old skin cream jars can be reused for salves and oils.
- Use organic or extra-virgin cold-pressed oils (make sure that they are not rancid).
- Beeswax can be purchased from local beekeepers or craft stores. You can also use the ends of old candles, as long as they are 100 percent beeswax. Give them a little rinse first.
- If you are adding essential oils to your salve, make sure they are pure essential oils, not "fragrances," which are often synthetic.

- Always label everything you make. You might think you will remember, but even after all these years, I still have to compost something every now and again that I did not label, because I forgot what it was. I like to use green painters' masking tape because it is easy to remove once I am done.

Medicine-making supplies.

Katrina Rainoshek

Glossary

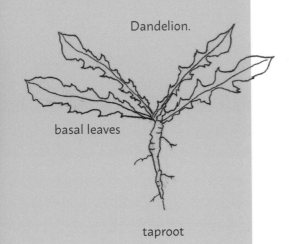

Dandelion.

basal leaves

taproot

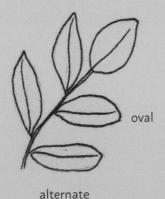

Red Huckleberry.

oval

alternate

acidic soil: soil that contains a lot of acid, often in dry forests and **bogs**

algae: plant-like organisms that contain chlorophyll but do not flower

alkaloid: naturally occurring chemical in plants

arid: dry

basal: growing from the base of the plant or stalk

biannual: a plant that flowers in its second year

bioregion: an area defined by shared plants and ecosystems

bog: a low wet area

botanist: someone who studies plants

bracts: a leaf of a tree or plant that looks like a petal

broad-leaved: a deciduous tree

buttress: a wide base that flares out to support trees or buildings

carnivore/carnivorous: a plant or animal that eats other creatures

catkins: the long dangling groups of small flowers on trees like Alder

cavity nester: a bird who builds its nest in a hole, either in a tree or a bank

clan: a subclass of a plant family (e.g., the *Rubus* clan)

colonization: when one group of people takes over and destroys the land and culture of another people

compostable: a natural material that will break down into tiny particles and turn back into the earth

conifer/coniferous: a tree or forest of trees that have needles or fronds, not leaves (e.g., Douglas Fir)

convulsions: extreme shaking

coppicing: a traditional method of harvesting wood without killing a tree

deciduous: a tree or herbaceous plant that loses its leaves in the autumn

disturbed: ground that has been changed from its original state by fire, road building, machinery or grazing

dormant: when a plant is not growing, often in winter or during a drought

ecosystem: an interaction between land, water, animals and plants that form an interdependent community

ecology: the study of the relationships between plants, their environment and each other; the specific place animals or plants live

elevation: the height the land is at compared with the ocean—a mountain is at high elevation; the beach is at low elevation

estuary: an area where a river flows into the ocean

ethical: something done with respect and care

evergreen: a tree or plant that stays green all year, with either needles or leaves

fertile: able to make new plants

frond: a large divided leaf, like that of a Fern or Cedar tree

fungi: the scientific word for mushrooms

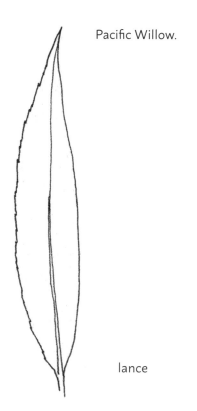

Pacific Willow.

lance

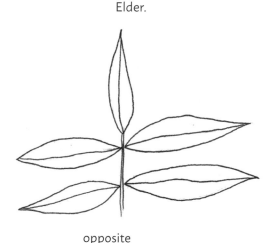

Elder.

opposite

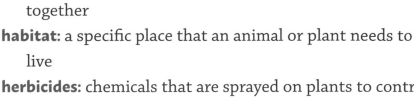
Maple.

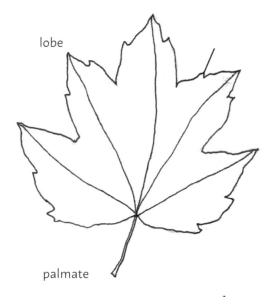
lobe

palmate

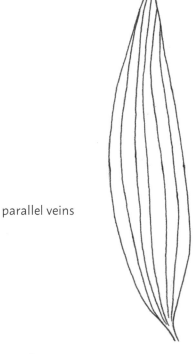
parallel veins

graft: a combining of two related plants so that they grow together

habitat: a specific place that an animal or plant needs to live

herbicides: chemicals that are sprayed on plants to control their growth or kill them

high elevation: growing either in the mountains or high inland from the sea

Indigenous: people who have lived in a place since time immemorial, long before settlers came from elsewhere; plants or animals that originated in an area

invasive plants: plants that come from a different area and take over the habitat of other plants

lance-shaped: leaves shaped like a spear tip or knife

leaf margins: the edges of the leaf

lichen: an organism that is made up of both algae and fungi

lobed: a leaf with round, bumpy edges

mycelium: the underground root-like parts of fungi that feed them and connect and communicate with the forest

nervous system: the part of your body in charge of all the movements you don't think about, like breathing and heartbeats; also in charge of how you sleep and respond to stress

node: the place where a leaf or stem attaches or grows from

northern hemisphere: the part of the earth that is north of the equator

nurse log: a dead tree on the forest floor that has baby trees growing from it

old-growth forest: a forest of very old trees that has never been logged

opposite: leaves that grow across from each other on the same stem

parallel veins: veins of a leaf that run straight next to one another

palmate: leaves shaped like the palm of a hand (e.g., Maple)

parasite: an animal or plant that lives off another animal or plant, often harming its host

perennial: a plant that lives for more than two years

pesticides: chemicals that are sprayed on insects to kill them

photosynthesis: the chemical process plants use to turn sunlight into food

plant guilds: plants that often grow together, like Douglas Fir and Salal

pollinator: an insect or animal that carries pollen from one flower to another

pollinating: when pollen from the male part of a plant mixes with the female part of a plant, producing fertile seeds that can then grow more plants

propagate: to make a new plant by cutting a piece from another plant and growing it out

rhizome: a root that travels underground with nodes that can sprout into new shoots of the plant

Oak.

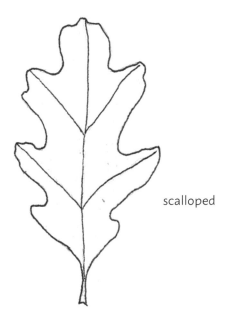

scalloped

Blueberry.

smooth

Trailing Blackberry.

toothed

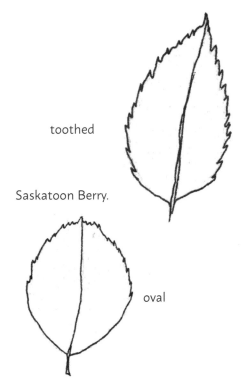

Saskatoon Berry.

oval

Chocolate Lily.

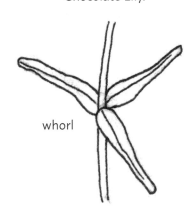

whorl

runners: like a rhizome but at the surface of the soil; a way for a plant to spread along the ground

scat: animal poop

sepals: the outer petal-like covering of the petals, often green under the petals

sori: a cluster of small spores on the underside of a Fern leaf

species: a way of organizing similar types of living creatures into groups

spores: the tiny cells that ferns, lichens and mosses use to reproduce

stamen: the part of the flower that produces pollen

sterile: not able to reproduce or make new plants

styptic: a plant that stops bleeding

subclass: a smaller group of plants within a plant family with shared characteristics

tannins: a reddish-coloured **alkaloid** found in some plants like Oak and Hemlock used to make dyes

umbels: umbrella-shaped flowers

understory: the plants that make up the forest beneath the trees

veins: the part of a leaf that moves water and food, often visible as lines in the leaf

volatile oils: natural chemicals in plants that have a strong smell and can be used as medicine

wildcrafting: harvesting plants for food or medicine in the wild

wildlife tree: an old tree with holes in it that animals use as a home or a food source

Plant Book Quiz

1. On page 28, there is a poisonous plant that is covered with yellow flowers when it blooms in spring. What is it?
2. Which plant has spade-shaped leaves and a spicy root?
3. What is one way to tell that a plant is from the Mint family?
4. What does the top of a Hemlock tree do?
5. What does the Latin name for Red Flowering Currant mean?
6. What is an easy way to identify Water Hemlock? Why is this so important?
7. Can you eat Thistles?
8. What is an important rule for harvesting plants?
9. On page 105, there is a plant that is good for Nettle stings, bee stings, cuts and scrapes. What is it?
10. What family are Huckleberry, Blueberry and Evergreen Huckleberry in?
11. What plant makes good hiker's toilet paper?
12. What are three knife safety tips?
13. There is a plant with berries on page 132. Which is okay to eat: red or blue?
14. Which plant is described as the "Walmart of the marsh"?
15. How many leaf shapes can you name?
16. Which plant can be used to make "coffee"?
17. Who combs their hair more, Douglas Fir or Grand Fir?

ANSWERS: 1. Scotch Broom; 2. Wild Ginger; 3. They have square stems; 4. It droops; 5. "Blood red"; 6. "Veins to the cut, hurt your gut." It is important to properly identify because it is poisonous! 7. Yes; 8. Never harvest more than one plant out of ten; 9. Plantain; 10. *Vaccinium*; 11. Mullein; 12. Make a "blood bubble," carve away from your body and stay sitting down; 13. Blue; 14. Cattail; 15. In this book we mention oval, spade, palmate, lobed and lance-shaped leaves; 16. Dandelion; 17. Grand Fir

Acknowledgements

The unfurling of a White Fawn Lily.

My deepest gratitude goes to the plants themselves and the lands, waters and animals that nourish them. Without these, nothing would be. I am hugely grateful to all those who work to keep our world healthy: the land, water and animal protectors and defenders, those on the front lines and those in the background. Thank you to those who keep stories, knowledge and tradition alive: the Elders of this place, the Indigenous people of the past and present whose long relationship with the land and plants has created such beauty and generosity. I feel deep respect for those who are working to restore and encourage culture and connection with the land. Without all this work, without all the stories and teachings handed down, we would have very little of this knowledge. I am grateful to the ancestors of this land, the people of this land and the descendants of this land for having me here. I acknowledge the loss and trauma that occurred on this land that has allowed me and other non-Indigenous people to make our homes here. Thank you to the K'ómoks, Pentlatch, Qualicum, Homalco, Klahoose, Tla'amin, We Wai Kai and Wei Wai Kum people of central "Vancouver Island," whose lands I live on now. Thank you to the Lekwungen, W̱SÁNEĆ, Musqueam, Squamish and

212

Tsleil-Waututh people, whose lands I have lived on in the past. These lands, waters and plants have nourished me and my family.

I have had many human teachers, and I thank them, especially Jasmyn Clift, Mimi Kamp and Nadine Ijaz. Some of my other human teachers are the kids I get to spend my days with at our outdoor school called Salix School on Sla-dai-aich, or Denman Island, where I live. "Salix" is the Latin name for Willow, which, like the kids, grows near water and is resilient and flexible. I learn so much through the wonderful curiosity, keen attention and endless questions of children.

Thank you to all the kids and youth who have learned about this beautiful world with me, and to the ones who are in the photos, including: AC, Akai, Alexander, Arawyn, Astrid, Astrud, Avery, Bella, Breah, Briar, Chantel, Chantel #2, Elli, Gabby, Harriet, Isabella, June, Louisena, Mae, Margret, Maya, Milliano, Naomi, Naya, Poet, Raphael, Rueben, Sarita, Sophia, Stella, Tosh, Westerly, Zaylia and Zemera.

Thank you to my family and my friends for your encouragement and support. Thanks to Jenna for your insights and editing. Thank you to Jason for our initial collaboration; I am sad you will never see the fruition of that inspiration. Finally, thank you to both my B's. Breah, you are my muse and the one I fight for the future for. Brad, you help me fly high and dive deep. I love you both.

Thank you to the wonderful editors and staff at Harbour Publishing for working with me on this project.

References and Suggested Reading

Print

Deur, Douglas. *Pacific Northwest Foraging: 120 Wild and Flavorful Edibles from Alaska Blueberries to Wild Hazelnuts*. New York, NY: Timber Press, 2014.

Elpel, Thomas J. *Botany in a Day: The Patterns Method of Plant Identification*. Pony, MT: HOPS Press, 1996.

Fenger, Mike, T. Manning, J. Cooper, S. Guy, and P. Bradford. *Wildlife and Trees in British Columbia*. Edmonton, AB: Lone Pine Publishing, 2006.

Moore, Michael. *Medicinal Plants of the Pacific West*. Santa Fe, NM: Red Crane Books, 1993.

Pojar, Jim, and Andy MacKinnon, eds. *Plants of Coastal British Columbia*. Edmonton, AB: Lone Pine Publishing, 1994.

Sibley, David Allen. *The Sibley Field Guide to Birds of Western North America*. New York, NY: Alfred A. Knopf, 2003.

Turner, Nancy J. *Ancient Pathways, Ancestral Knowledge: Ethnobotany and Ecological Wisdom of Indigenous Peoples of Northwestern North America*. Montreal, QC: McGill-Queen's Press, 2014.

Turner, Nancy J. *Food Plants of Coastal First Peoples*. Victoria, BC: Royal BC Museum, 1995.

Wall Kimmerer, Robin. *Braiding Sweetgrass: Indigenous Wisdom, Scientific Knowledge and the Teachings of Plants*. Minneapolis, MN: Milkweed Editions, 2015.

Online

Indian Horse. "Next150 Challenge: Decolonized Landscapes." next150.indianhorse.ca/challenges/decolonized-landscapes

Native Land Digital. "Territory Acknowledgement." native-land.ca/resources/territory-acknowledgement/

The Canadian Encyclopedia. "Indigenous Territory," by Molly Malone and Libby Chisholm. thecanadianencyclopedia.ca/en/article/indigenous-territory

Index

About the Author

Philippa Joly is a clinical and community herbalist, paramedic and outdoor educator. She runs an outdoor school for kids and leads workshops on herbal medicine, plant identification, ethical wildcrafting, herbal first aid, local healing plants and anticolonial approaches to wellness. She lives on Denman Island, BC, with her plant-savvy daughter, Breah, and their grey cat. If you want to find out more or write Philippa a letter, visit her website: philippajoly.com.

Copyright © 2023 Philippa Joly

1 2 3 4 5 — 27 26 25 24 23

All rights reserved. No part of this publication may be reproduced, stored in a retrieval system or transmitted, in any form or by any means, without prior permission of the publisher or, in the case of photocopying or other reprographic copying, a licence from Access Copyright, www.accesscopyright.ca, 1-800-893-5777, info@accesscopyright.ca.

Harbour Publishing Co. Ltd.
P.O. Box 219, Madeira Park, BC, V0N 2H0
www.harbourpublishing.com

All photographs by Philippa Joly
     except where otherwise noted.
Edited by Sarah Harvey
Indexed by Emma Biron
Cover and text design by Libris Simas Ferraz /
     Onça Publishing
Cover photography: Top right by Katrina Rainoshek.
     All others by the author.
Illustrations by Philippa Joly
Printed and bound in South Korea
Printed with vegetable-based ink on paper certified by
the Forest Stewardship Council®

Harbour Publishing acknowledges the support of the Canada Council for the Arts, the Government of Canada, and the Province of British Columbia through the BC Arts Council.

Library and Archives Canada
Cataloguing in Publication
Title: A kid's guide to plants of the Pacific Northwest :
     with cool facts, activities and recipes / Philippa Joly.
Other titles: Plants of the Pacific Northwest
Names: Joly, Philippa, author.
Description: Includes bibliographical references
     and index.
Identifiers: Canadiana (print) 20230131166 |
     Canadiana (ebook) 20230131174 |
     ISBN 9781990776212 (softcover) |
     ISBN 9781990776229 (EPUB)
Subjects: LCSH: Plants—Northwest, Pacific—
     Identification—Juvenile literature. |
     LCSH: Plants—Northwest, Pacific—Juvenile
     literature. | LCSH: Botany—Northwest, Pacific—
     Juvenile literature. | LCGFT: Field guides. |
     LCGFT: Activity books.
Classification: LCC QK143 .J65 2023 |
     DDC j581.9795—dc23